70 SECRETS REVEALED

How To Write Content That Converts 600% More

Munmi Sarma
&
Harshajyoti Das

Copyright © 2013 by Harshajyoti Das

All rights reserved. No part of this publication may be reproduced in any form or by any means, including scanning, photocopying, or otherwise without prior written permission of the copyright holder.

Disclaimer and Terms of Use:

The Author and Publisher has strived to be as accurate and complete as possible in the creation of this book, notwithstanding the fact that he does not warrant or represent at any time that the contents within are accurate due to the rapidly changing nature of the Internet.

While all attempts have been made to verify information provided in this publication, the Author and Publisher assumes no responsibility for errors, omissions, or contrary interpretation of the subject matter herein. Any perceived slights of specific persons, peoples, or organizations are unintentional.

In practical advice books, like anything else in life, there are no guarantees of income made. Readers are cautioned to rely on their own judgment about their individual circumstances and act accordingly.

This book is not intended for use as a source of legal, business, accounting or financial advice. All readers are advised to seek services of competent professionals in the legal, business, accounting, and finance fields.

There some affiliate links in the content. This means that if you happen to buy anything through these links, I will get a commission from the seller. My intention is not to make sales. I have personally used these products and loved them. Please do your research before making a purchase.

Your FREE GIFTS

This is my first book, and I wholeheartedly thank you for purchasing it.

As a gesture of appreciation, I would like to offer you some **Free Bonus Gifts**.

http://fireyourmentor.com/free-bonus-3-gifts-with-my-book/

GIFT 1: **GUIDE:** *How to Automate Twitter*

I personally use all the techniques mentioned in this twitter guide. You can easily get 1000 followers in 10 days. Take it as my guarantee.

Gift 2: **GUIDE:** *An Introduction to Yellow Hat SEO*

Never heard of Yellow Hat SEO before? Well, that's because I have coined the term just recently. This guide contains tips on how you can use my Yellow Hat strategy to gain rankings without worrying about Google penalties.

Gift 3: **GUIDE:** *How to Copy Competitors' Back links*

This guide shows you the easiest way to search for your competitor's backlinks and build the same on your website – all in just 30 minutes.

This book is dedicated to each and every person who has given up their day job to start an entrepreneurial career.

ACKNOWLEDGEMENT:

Thank you for taking the time out of your busy schedule to read my book. I sincerely appreciate your endeavor to learn more about creating conversion boosting content.

I would like to thank my wife, *'Munmi Sarma',* for spending countless sleepless nights to help me finish and finally publish this book.

Thank you, Almighty, for giving me this beautiful life.

I am thankful to Amazon & Kindle for creating such a brilliant platform for self-publishing.

Special thanks to those who have always discouraged me from becoming an independent soul, an entrepreneur, an author. Your discouragement has helped me realized that I was up for something big.

"When people discourage you to do something, it's because they can't do it."

Table of Contents

Introduction

About the Authors

CHAPTER 1: Less is more
CHAPTER 2: Showcase your benefits
CHAPTER 3: Choose the right words
CHAPTER 4: Use contemporary designs
CHAPTER 5: Be profound and unambiguous
CHAPTER 6: Your content should resonate well with your readers
CHAPTER 7: Make your content visually appealing
CHAPTER 8: Target your reader's doubts
CHAPTER 9: Use images to induce credibility
CHAPTER 10: Get your visitors hooked
CHAPTER 12: Place your best content on top
CHAPTER 13: Illuminate significant content
CHAPTER 14: Ask fewer questions
CHAPTER 15: Conduct usability tests rapidly
CHAPTER 16: Demonstrate your accreditations and accomplishments
CHAPTER 17: Incorporate a sales pitch
CHAPTER 18: Embed audio and video into your content
CHAPTER 19: Add testimonials and other social proofs
CHAPTER 20: Call to action
CHAPTER 21: Publish and upgrade fresh content frequently
CHAPTER 22: Make use of bullet points
CHAPTER 23: Conduct split tests frequently
CHAPTER 24: Embed a demonstrative video
CHAPTER 25: Conduct a follow up
CHAPTER 26: Don't offer discounts
CHAPTER 27: Evaluate website metrics
CHAPTER 28: Limit the clicks between the sales page and the order page

CHAPTER 29: Unclutter your home page
CHAPTER 30: Back up your claims with proofs
CHAPTER 31: Accelerate your shipping process
CHAPTER 32: Get to the bottom line fast
CHAPTER 33: Accommodate a free trail button
CHAPTER 34: Offer product images
CHAPTER 35: Always offer extensive guarantees
CHAPTER 36: Promote list building
CHAPTER 37: Integrate red hyperlinks
CHAPTER 38: Offer giveaways
CHAPTER 39: Embed your phone number into the homepage
CHAPTER 40: Add context to all your products
CHAPTER 41: Offer premium options
CHAPTER 42: Simplify your checkout process
CHAPTER 43: Provide live support
CHAPTER 44: Include customer photos on your homepage
CHAPTER 45: Make use of Google optimizer
CHAPTER 46: Include pop-up & sign-up forms
CHAPTER 47: Invoke the human emotions
CHAPTER 48: Brush up your copywriting skills
CHAPTER 49: Borrow credibility
CHAPTER 50: Accumulate user reviews
CHAPTER 51: Provide product FAQ
CHAPTER 52: Evaluate your usp
CHAPTER 53: Have a sound returns policy
CHAPTER 54: Select a mobile responsive website
CHAPTER 55: Inform the customer every step of the way
CHAPTER 56: Price anchoring
CHAPTER 57: Test your products
CHAPTER 58: Reflect people's expectations
CHAPTER 59: Eliminate friction words
CHAPTER 60: Override all risks
CHAPTER 61: Announce the problem
CHAPTER 62: Serve your solution
CHAPTER 63: Clarity trumps persuasion

CHAPTER 64: Hire a visual designer
CHAPTER 65: Be specific
CHAPTER 66: Be exclusive
CHAPTER 67: Use triggers below the buttons
CHAPTER 68: Get a professional logo
CHAPTER 69: Leverage the convenience factor
CHAPTER 70: Write short sentences and paragraph

INTRODUCTION

This is the first book of a three-book series.

1. 70 Secrets Revealed: How To Write Content That Converts 600% More
2. 70 Secrets Revealed: Do Your Own SEO Better than 'SEO Experts'
3. 70 Secrets Revealed: Social Media Strategies That Nobody Will Teach You.

I understand the pain of not being able to convert website visitors into customers. It's really frustrating.

I have been in your shoes several times in the past when I used to run multiple affiliate sites. I kept trying new strategies to engage and convert these visitors. That's how I learned what works and what don't.

This book was written with the sole intention of helping people who want to learn more about writing on the web and converting visitors into customers. Most people don't know the difference between writing for a website and writing for a magazine.

If you are already a veteran in internet marketing, you can use this book as a reference to create a new website or a new sales page.

Even if you take away 10% of the knowledge in this book, you will learn a lot more than 90% of the people who have an online business.

All right, if you are in front of a computer, please open your website, blog or a landing page.

The best way to read this book is to open your website or a sales page and cross-reference with this book. You can fix a lot of loopholes on your website that are often overlooked.

Within a few minutes, I will take you through *70 ways to make your content better on your website*. You will be able to connect better with your visitors. Your visitors will love and trust your work. As expected, it's not really easy to win someone's trust online. Once you do it right, you will be able to convert these visitors into loyal customers.

At the end of each chapter, you will find something called, **"Take Away"**. *I like to think of them as phrases that stick to your brain.*

I am always happy to help. If you have any queries or suggestions regarding this book, you can reach me at harsh@fireyourmentor.com. I check my email twice a week and try to reply to as many emails as I can.

Twitter: @jr_sci

FB Page: https://www.facebook.com/FireYourMentor

GOOGLE+:
https://plus.google.com/+HarshajyotiDas/posts

About the Authors

The Husband and Wife duo makes a living by working on the internet from the comfort of their home. They try to help others achieve the same.

Munmi Sarma

Munmi is the Chairperson and Co-Founder of Munmi IT Solutions LLP. She is a globetrotter, painter, blogger, life coach and entrepreneur. She tries to pen down the *'Enigma of Life'* at her blog, Penigma.com

Harshajyoti Das

Harsh is the CEO and Co-Founder of Munmi IT Solutions LLP.

He is a traveler, a writer, an inbound marketer (SEO'er), an entrepreneur, and a business adviser.

He helps upcoming entrepreneurs by offering them motivational tips and internet marketing advice on his blog, FireYourMentor.com

Chapter 1

LESS IS MORE

It is very tempting to fill your site with a lot of information, but you should never forget that visitors will simply hit the 'back' button if they do not comprehend the information.

Simplify and shorten all your content. Minimize the number of forms that need to be filled. Eliminate all unnecessary requests and data.

Reduce unnecessary data such as ads, opt-in forms, sidebars, etc. However, you do need to have detailed product descriptions, FAQs, testimonials and sound information about you and your company. Focus on what your visitors want to see instead of what you want to show them.

You need to cover more topics with less content. People tend to assume that 'more is better', but the fact is, lengthy product lists are conversion killers. If you want to increase your conversions by 600%, you have to streamline all your offerings.

Purchasing products or services is a strenuous job. You need to comprehend the given information, compare it with the competitors' products, assess if the product matches your requirements and finally make the decision to purchase it or not. So, if you have a painstakingly long and complicated product list, your prospects will have to undergo the aforementioned decision-making process for every item, and that's a back-breaking task.

I am not suggesting that you eliminate products; I am simply stating that streamlining your offers will drastically increase your conversions.

Let me explain this further with an example:

Let's take two examples. In both examples, the word count of the book will remain the same.

I have covered **70 Topics** in this book. Each topic is short and precise. I could have written *just 10 topics* that are 10-15 pages long.

Which one would you have preferred?

Take Away This: *Save Time*

Chapter 2

SHOWCASE YOUR BENEFITS

Customers are always very eager to find out how they will benefit from your site. Hence, fill your homepage with compelling and convincing benefits. Be extremely precise and profound while exhibiting all your benefits. Make use of persuasive language while doing so.

Mailchimp.com does it pretty well with their Slider.

Benefits can involve a wide range of things. Specify how your product can change a person's life. You can also take notes from your testimonials or reviews and highlight them under 'how this product has helped real customers'. People tend to follow. If you show (with enough evidence) that your product has benefited other customers, they are most likely to buy your product as well.

Your site is a visitor's first glimpse at your services and products. Obviously, if they don't appreciate what they read or see, they will go someplace else. People buy a product because it is a solution to their problem. It's wise if you can combine benefit-selling with solution-selling; that way, your prospects will understand how your product is better than the competition.

Figure out all the reasons why your customers buy from you, and mention those elements in your first paragraph. Try to craft a benefit-focused description. Using attention-grabbing headlines and highlighting benefits will further foster positive feelings towards your products.
A couple of days back, a guy came to me and asked why his visitors were not converting. Most people who visited his site stayed hardly for 2-3 seconds. I checked his website, and here's what I found:

Instead of showing how his products can benefit his customers, he was more interested in selling, putting price quotes and placing 'buy now' buttons.

I scrolled to the bottom of his website and found that he also had a free product. He could have simply put that free product at the top of his website and captured those leads. People will automatically convert if he provides value. They need to understand **how** a product or a service can benefit them.

People are eager to pay you if you can solve their problem. Showcase your benefits; tell them **HOW** your product can solve their problem.

Take Away This: *Focus on 'How'*

Chapter 3

CHOOSE THE RIGHT WORDS

Selecting the right words will make a huge difference. Do not use complicated and uncommon words. Be smooth-tongued and use coaxing words. Convey the message to your visitors directly, and do not use distracting language. Incorporate interactive, intriguing and dynamic content.

It might be a good idea to experiment a little in the beginning and see which article gets more social shares and comments. You can try to be either formal or casual. You can write a humorous article or an in-depth, well-researched article. Once you have figured out what your audience is really looking for, you can continue writing in that vein.

There are four magic words that can boost your conversions tremendously. These words have been defined in psychology, neuro-economics and behavioral economics to appeal to a customer's primal instincts.

These words are:

You: It's the most commanding word in the English language. For marketers, it's much more influential than words like 'sales' or 'money'. We might not admit it, but we all are a bit egocentric. When product descriptions focus directly on us, a very powerful connection is created subconsciously.

New: When people see the word 'new', they subconsciously relate it to something innovative, improved, exciting and adventurous. According to many studies, new products or services draw many customers with the 'new' label. For example, Apple describes the iPhone 5's design as a 'New' design, with 'New' technology for their 'New' iPhone.

Free: The word 'free' doesn't only have price connotations; it's also a very dominant emotional trigger and generates a lot of implausible excitement. The word 'free' is a very powerful conversion boosting word. Amazon has used the full potential of the word 'free'.

They keep perfecting their marketing strategies to take advantage of our thirst for 'free' products.

Guaranteed: The word 'guarantee' is the ultimate key component of most good sales copies. It generates feelings of security and trust in customers. It's also a safety net that assures the customers that they will be very satisfied with their purchase. People are instinctively terrified of loss. Guaranteeing the customer's purchase reduces the possibility of loss.

Take Away This: *Words makes a difference*

Chapter 4

USE CONTEMPORARY DESIGNS

Use modern day designs. Do not make your site look like it's from the 80's. Contemporary designs will attract and engage visitors. Modernizing the site has many advantages; it boosts credibility, appeals to new users, fascinates visitors and leaves a prolonged and positive impact in their minds.

Contemporary designs increase the conversion ratio of a particular website. Designs are not only about making the site spectacular; they are also about making a site rewarding and profitable. A site should not be built only from an aesthetic perspective; you have to start considering traffic, profits and conversion ratios.

Conversions should be the basic focus of all websites; if a site doesn't convert, it has to be shut down. It is difficult to design a site that easily attains a high conversion rate, but putting a design strategy in place becomes comparatively easier if improving conversions is the paramount focus.

Always design for the visitors or users. Try to make your design instinctive, so that your visitors don't have to think about their next move. The user flow of your site must be flawless. Make it extremely easy for the user to navigate from point A to point B. They should be able to navigate effortlessly. By enhancing the usability of your site, you can contribute towards informed decision-making, which ultimately leads to better conversions.

Your visitors are impatient and have a very short attention span, so your site should be designed in such a way that it can offer the maximum amount of information in a very short time. Allow your first-time visitors to go through your site quickly, and do not force them to fill in overly long forms. Design a trustworthy website so that apart from the reviews, ratings and testimonials, the design makes them trust the site.

You can easily use your site's design to promote or project your credibility. You can achieve this by focusing on a clean and precise design that doesn't confuse and comes straight to the point. If you try too hard to increase your conversions, this pushiness may at times be reflected very strongly in your design. In such cases, your visitors may find it hard to trust your site. So, keep it simple, because nothing works better than simplicity when ensuring an increased conversion rate.

What are the factors that you look for in a website? (Hint: check http://unbounce.com)

- A site must be responsive (phone/tablet-friendly).
- Utilize the full screen.
- Build trust and try to accomplish it on the first page.
- Have an 'Action Button' above the Fold.

Invest in a good design, because it will show results within a very short time. If you are using WordPress, you can get a ready-made theme from Theme Forest (http://fireyourmentor.com/theme-forest) for as low as $25.

Take Away This: *Use designs that are in trend.*

Chapter 5

BE PROFOUND AND UNAMBIGIOUS

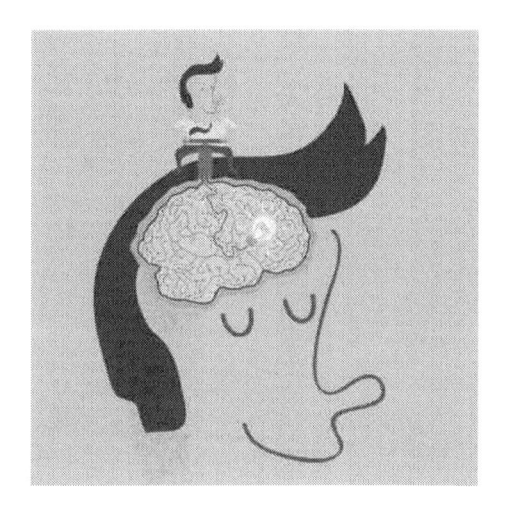

Use clear, simple, well-defined and straightforward information. Confirm that your customers comprehend the message completely and without much difficulty. Make sure that your content is not generating confusion, chaos or disarray.

This might seem too simple, but apparently, it is very hard for some sites to get it right. The more difficult and chaotic you make your site, the less conversions you will get. Try to present the information in such a way that it can prevent nobody from buying. Always be open and honest; if a product is out of stock, state it directly. Finding out that a product is not available after reading all the information about it and adding it to the cart can be very annoying.

You have to be more sincere when you describe your pricing strategies; a user will most likely not continue the sale if after spending $150 on a particular product, they find out that shipping is an extra $100. It can be a little tricky to divulge delivery pricing, but it's definitely not impossible.

Your content should be straight to the point and should help your customers to 'solve a problem'. Let me explain. A person often comes online to find a solution to a particular problem. Say, for example, someone is searching for symptoms of a stomach ulcer or a home remedy for a cold. This person is looking for immediate access to the solution to his problem; he doesn't want to go through paragraphs of irrelevant material to get to the solution. Your content should therefore be straight to the point and should help your customers to solve a problem.

Confront the problem directly. Google has recently started revealing comprehensive articles called, "in-depth articles" on Search Results. If you read these informative articles carefully, you will notice that they are very thorough and not superficial. They offer elaborate information. They also include references to tons of relevant sources that you can link back to so that your readers can examine further to find more information on that particular topic.

Recently, I read an article on Rohit Palit's blog (http://fireyourmentor.com/techtage) that had **over 10k words**. This blog post received 99% better response than any of his previous articles (in terms of email sign-ups, comments, shares, etc).

Take Away This: *Readers should think you are a genius when you write.*

Chapter 6

YOUR CONTENT SHOULD RESONATE WELL WITH YOUR READERS

The words or language used should match, correspond to, or represent people's interests and needs. If the content resonates well with your readers, then you will be more effective in converting them into customers. Describe in detail exactly what people are searching for. Focus on their needs in order to grab their attention.

Creating content that resonates well with all your readers is a critical and complex task to master. Content that strikes a chord with your readers is the stuff that gets forwarded, shared and linked to other sites. It's what forces people to read till the end and drives conversions.
It enhances your marketing from ordinary to stupendous. There are certain essential elements that need to be correctly infused into you content to make it relatable and much more impactful.

You have to identify your audience in order to create content that resonates with them. Put in the effort to develop personas, i.e., buyer personas; however, in addition to buyer personas, you will also have to create 'reader personas'. It is very important that you create reader personas because, other than readers who generally convert into customers, there is also a separate group of readers who might never buy from your site, but will continue to share and read your content. When you conduct the persona research, you will eventually find the right elements that need to be infused into your content.

Always present content in the right format, and decide which content format type is the best to get your message across. You could decide to embed a video instead of a manual, an info-graphic instead of a blog post; you have to determine what content format will keep your audience engrossed. Info-graphics are very powerful, as they combine imagery, words and numbers to portray a message. Try to use data to support your content. Sometimes you need mathematics to convey the significance of a point; the numbers mostly speak for themselves.

There's a very thin line between writing for the targeted audience and for the wrong audience. Let me explain this further with the help of an example: Let's say, you have a blog about 'Dog Training' and you are trying to sell an e-book on "How to Train Your Dog in 4 Weeks". When you are writing a sales copy for your blog, if you focus more on telling them why they should train their dog rather than explaining how, there are less chances of your content being appreciated.

Identify the problem first. Here, the main problem seems to be that they don't know how to train their dog. At the same time, they don't want to take their dog to a professional trainer. They want to train their dog right at home. It will be a good idea to offer the first two chapters for free and then eventually show them how the whole book can help them to solve their problem.

Take Away This: *Tell them what they want to hear, not what you want to say.*

Chapter 7

MAKE YOUR CONTENT VISUALLY APPEALING

To increase your rapport or resonance with your customers, make your content visually gratifying. Demonstrate and depict people's desires through images, charts, and other visual stimulants. This technique is very effective in boosting conversions, as it invokes a psychological response in customers.

Your site is where you house all the important information about your products and services, and it is where all your visitors end up validating your brand credibility. First impressions are very significant; they may cause you to lose or win a particular sale. However, you get a very limited time to make a great first impression.

Generally, your visitors give around 8 seconds to your website, and within that time, they decide whether to continue reading about the product or service that they are looking for. So, your site needs to be visually appealing and informative to help your visitors determine in those 8 seconds whether your site is useful or not. A visually appealing site might be the determining factor for increasing conversions.

To design a site that attracts your target audience, consider the following points:

• **Never overuse animated images.** Animated images can convert an ordinary site into something innovative. However, overusing them can make your site very confusing, and ultimately, they may do more harm than good.

• **Find the right balance between texts and graphics.** You have to use graphics to make your site visual, but make sure you include the adequate amount of text on your site to help your visitors comprehend what your business is all about. The key is about finding the right balance between the two.

• **Place your CTA button above the fold.** Any CTA (Call to Action) button should be very prominent, and preferably, above the fold, so that your visitors can easily locate it. Don't keep your visitors looking for the button.

Think about an article with no image, no video, no sub-headings and no bullet points! There's simply no way you can retain a reader on that page for more than 30 seconds. This will directly affect the 'bounce rate' on your website. Google considers 'bounce rate' to be one of the main ranking factors in their search algorithm.

Note: "Bounce rate" is a term used in Google Analytics which indicates if a person bounces off from a page without reading it.

Your potential customers will definitely judge a book by its cover, and you cannot afford to lose customers just because your site failed to attract them. Design and content go hand in hand, so make the necessary amends to your design to lure visitors to read your content.

Here are certain guidelines I personally follow while writing my articles. You can copy them and send them to your writer.

- Sub-headings (h2)
- Sub-sub headings (h3)
- Bullets and numbering
- Paragraphs should be precise(3-4 lines)
- Sentences should be short(10-20 words)
- One image beside every point, analysis or interpretation
- At least 1 video per article
- At least 3 images per article (400 px)
- Quotes and catchphrases wherever applicable, along

with a ClickToTweet button. (http://fireyourmentor.com/click-to-tweet)
- Names of people, important words and phrases in bold letters

Take Away This: *Websites shouldn't irritate your eyes.*

Chapter 8

ADDRESS YOUR READER'S DOUBTS

Generally, visitors are skeptical and unsure about your execution, operation, implementation and deliverance. Hence, focus on clearing away their doubts. Do not ignore or neglect their uncertainties. Explain what they are signing up for. Convinced and satisfied visitors are more likely to convert.

A recent study showed that 26% of the people surveyed had trust issues and constantly worried about sharing their personal security data and credit card information.

You cannot completely eliminate the trust issue with your online customers, but you can definitely diminish it so that most of your visitors take the much-needed action.

It is not so simple to make someone who has never seen you or met you to whip out their credit cards. However, if you follow certain tips carefully, you can easily make more people start clicking your call-to-action buttons. Set up a proper 'About Me' page that contains information about you and your credentials. Readers can then feel like they can connect with you; if they don't know who they're doing business with, they may never return.

Email marketing is another good approach. A study conducted by "Sales Force" showed that 44% of email recipients make at least one purchase. You can also post interviews with experts in your field. If you do this frequently, you will definitely increase your traffic and your conversion rates.

Accumulate expert product reviews

They are somewhat similar to testimonials, but these product reviews carry more weight because they come from experts who have tried your product, like a thought leader or a famous blogger in your niche. Always have a 'Privacy Policy' on your site because a privacy policy is a legitimate legal document that can increase your conversions from 3% to 30%. Without a privacy policy, you will have a very tough time convincing a customer to make a purchase.

Most people lose their customers on the 'Check Out' page because they don't address their doubts. If you are selling something via your website, you should list a phone number on each and every page of your website. That way, whenever a potential buyer has doubts, he or she can easily find your number and call you before going through the purchasing process.

Make sure you have a FAQ (Frequently Asked Question) page on your site. It will help you to address your reader's doubts correctly.

The best way to prepare a FAQ is to put yourself in your reader's shoes. Write down at least 20 points that will define your own skepticism as a reader. It can be anything ranging from shipping terms, shipping costs, delivery time, refund terms, payment methods, credit card security, product guarantees or privacy policies.

Another important technique is to use a 'Live Help' feature on your website. There are free softwares provided by companies like Zopim.com that you can easily install on your website with a simple javascript. Your readers can then contact you or your customer service department directly via Live Chat. You can also integrate popular messengers like Gtalk.

If you are writing a blog, try to focus on solving people's problems by writing more "How To" articles. You will receive a better response with these than with articles on topics that are too broad and general.

Matthew Woodward has reportedly earned more than **$73,000 within 12 months** with his brand new blog (http://fireyourmentor.com/matthew-woodward). How did he do it? He focused on solving people's problems by answering common questions in his niche.

Take Away This: *Don't let a visitor leave your site with a query in their mind.*

Chapter 9

USE IMAGES TO INDUCE CREDIBILITY

Images foster credibility, conversions, trustworthiness, and believability. A picture paints a thousand words. Use unique and pertinent images that attract your target audience. They will not only enhance the quality and caliber of the content, but will also make the content captivating, charismatic and enchanting. They reduce buyer resistance.

Most people never buy anything before seeing it. Moreover, they usually want to touch it or simply hold it. Since it is not possible to do such things online, you need to work thrice as hard to make your products convincingly appealing.

Always embed high quality images and clickable thumbnails; a lot of websites try to sell products with very low-quality images. Include images of the product from different angles; that way, your potential customers can easily get a feel of it.

Don't simply show the product; try to show it in context. It's best to avoid stock photos, because when it comes to images, real people or real photos get a lot more attention than stock photos. It's wise to embed 360-degree rotating images.

DueMaternity.com boosted their conversions by 27% by using two dimensional images on their site. Using human photos on your landing page can also increase your conversions significantly. Medalia Art, a company that sells Brazilian art online, increased their conversions by 95% by using photos of their artists on their homepage. Always use photos of real people, and never opt for the cheesy stock photos.

Using good quality images in your blog posts can easily increase your sales because images enhance readability and upgrade the user experience. Obviously, the posts that are without images tend to be boring and contribute towards less reading.

I will give you an example. There are two 'statements' below. Which one is more convincing?

Example 1:

My E-book will teach you to take photographs like a professional. Risk-free 30 days money back guarantee. Buy it now for only $14.95

Example 2:

My E-book will teach you to take photographs like a professional. Risk-free 30 days money back guarantee. Buy it now for only $14.95

Obviously, the second example is more convincing because the image induces credibility.

People tend to believe what they see more than what they read or listen. Whenever you want to make a statement, embed an image beside your text. It will invoke a psychological response in your readers.

According to Derek Halpern founder of Social Triggers, (http://fireyourmentor.com/social-triggers), a top marketing blog, images can convince people a lot better than simple text. On a personal note, I have learnt a lot from him. If you haven't watched his videos, then you definitely should.

Take Away This: *Use images. I can't be more concise than this.*

Chapter 10

GET YOUR VISITORS HOOKED

The deepest human desire is to be understood. Hence, leverage it. 'Empathy' is a very powerful sales tool. Empathize with your reader's problems and agonies. Acknowledge their concerns and eradicate their objections and dissents.

Human beings are all predictably emotional; we are afraid of the dark and like to cuddle. Marketers use human psychology to their advantage to persuade consumers to buy products or services. All human beings are comprised of id, ego and super-ego, and our logic raises many questions and doubts, but our emotion lowers them. Emotional appeal always surpasses intellectual appeal. A recent study has further proved that 'non-rational influence' is more powerful than 'rational persuasion'.

'Empathy' can be your most powerful productivity tool. It is a valued currency that allows the site to create trust and credibility. There are tons of studies that relate 'empathy' to 'increased conversions'. It has given rise to new terms such as 'empathy selling' or 'empathy marketing'. Try to create an empathy map, which is a map that describes your target audience's point of view.

Creating an empathy map is about creating a map of their perspective, so that you can understand them better. This map helps you to fill in gaps of all the necessary information that you are missing about your audience.

You need to empathize with your potential customers, and this requires more than simply putting yourself in your customer's shoes. Empathy is the ability to describe what your potential customers feel about their challenges.

It is very important to speak the language of your customers, as it is a good strategy in your marketing campaign. You have to adequately satisfy your customer's emotional needs. You have to smartly add certain emotional elements to your marketing strategies.

Empathetic marketing should be part of your marketing endeavor.

How do you feel when someone says these two magical words, 'I understand'?

You need to implement a sense of empathy in your words to convey them that 'you understand' their problems or worries. Let me give you an example; envision that you are selling an anti-aging product. Which sales pitch will have the maximum impact on your readers?

Example 1:

Our anti-aging cream will hide all your wrinkles within just 3 minutes after applying it. It has worked for hundreds of others and will work for you as well. It's the best available anti-aging cream in the market today.

Example 2:

I understand that it's hard to step out in public with your wrinkles. You want to look young and fresh. We have designed our product while keeping customers like you in mind. It just takes 3 minutes after application to remove all your wrinkles.

Evidently, Example 2 is the clear winner. It creates a connection with the readers by showing 'empathy' and identifying with their problem. I did a split test with these two sales copies for one of my clients who sell beauty products. **Example 2** made **60% more sales** than **Example 1**.

__Take Away This:__ *Showing empathy will take you a long way.*

Chapter 11

WRITE CATCHY HEADLINES

The headline should be arousing and conjuring. It should depict the customer's needs and also address the customer's objections. It should be short and simple. It should be clear, distinct and definite. It should be attention grabbing and comprehensible at the same time.

The headline is probably the most crucial selling point. When a visitor visits your website, the first thing that catches their eye is the headline. If it doesn't entice them, they will close their browser even before scrolling down and reading the rest of your site. You get a few seconds to pique your visitor's interest, so spend some time creating the perfect headline.

A headline should solve a problem. It should talk about your "Unique Selling Proposition". A great headline can do much more than simply grabbing someone's attention; it can be used to communicate a message to the target audience. A persuasive headline should promise a certain reward or benefit to the reader, in exchange for his or her time.

Mint.com has done it so well. It's a software that helps you keep track of your budget. If you visit their website, you will see this headline: ***"It's easy to understand what's going on with your money."***

There are tons of other examples. Mixergy (http://fireyourmentor.com/mixergy), which interviews entrepreneurs who have already built a successful business, has a headline that says, ***"Learn From Proven Entrepreneurs".*** Tid.al, a platform for guest bloggers and contributors, has a very simple yet compelling headline that says, ***"Tidal connects individuals to top brands and publishers"***

Try to write an effective headline and a persuasive sales pitch. Your headline is the only way to entice your visitors to continue reading. It has only one purpose — to make the reader move on to the next line. Try to convey your value proposition and also describe your product smartly with your headline. It's no good if it does not spark enough interest. You might spend days creating the best sales page, but no one will ever read it if it does not have a solid headline.

Take Away This: *A headline defines your entire website.*

Chapter 12

PLACE YOUR BEST CONTENT ON TOP

Be ruthless with the top part of your site. Select your most persuasive, credible, diligent content and place it on the top. The top part is the only space that gets maximum exposure and attention; hence, fill it up with convincing content. Prove your caliber through it and do not fill it up with draggy, uninteresting or uninspiring information. It will chase your visitors away.

If you do not address usability and design issues, then

you are simply wasting your time, no matter how good your content is. You have to balance content with design for increased conversions. Your visitors will judge your site even before making the first click. Their instant reaction determines whether they will continue reading or leave. Most people only focus on the top part of the site known as 'above the fold'. So, place your best content up top. You have to meticulously use the area above the fold to motivate your customers to read further.

About 40-50% of your visitors leave after seeing just a single page. Imagine, if half of your traffic disappears, your conversions will decline rapidly. According to a recent report by ClickTale, the top part of a page gets 19 times more exposure than the bottom part. Hence, anything newsworthy or significant needs to be above the page fold.

Less than 50% of your visitors will scroll down to check the rest of your content. The first thing they will see is the headline. Then you have your offer with a CTA (call to action) button. Now, let's see what comes below the fold.

You will have content, graphs, videos, slide shows, sales pitches, FAQs, and pricing tables below the fold. You need to put the best content on the top. Conversions are expected to rise **by 200%** if you have the best content on top.

Check what Zopim (http://fireyourmentor.com/zopim) has done. They have a simple headline that directly confronts a customer's problem. Then they have a slideshow that demonstrates its features. Their slideshow is one of the key elements in attracting new customers. Below the fold, they have a short 'about us' paragraph, followed by quotes and testimonials.

Take Away This: *"Above the fold" is your secret goldmine.*

Chapter 13

ILLUMINATE SIGNIFICANT CONTENT

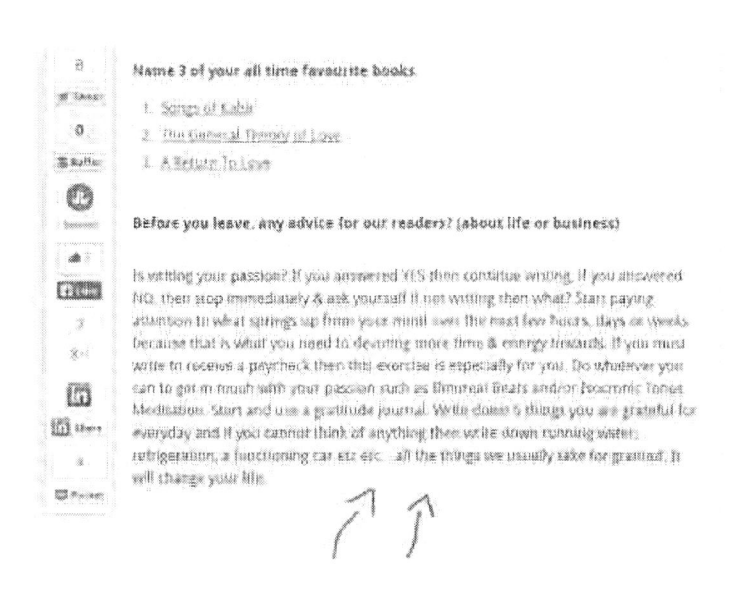

Illuminate or elucidate essential content. This will attract visitors and they will be lured by it. Any content that has profound value or significance should be perceptibly exhibited. It should be highlighted clearly, in order to grab the visitor's attention.

A great design focuses on highlighting your crucial content. Every service or product has its own USP

(Unique selling proposition). Spend some time researching your competitor's products, then highlight your USP in **bold**. If your product or service is the very first of its kind, focus on the word 'new'. You can also highlight your product's 'guarantees' because a guarantee suggests trustworthiness and makes buying decisions much easier.

You need to have something bewitching in your content that will grab the attention of your readers and compel them to continue reading. When you put quotes in your article, make them tweet to clickable using (http://fireyourmentor.com/click-to-tweet) . Remember, quotes are the most tweeted and re-tweeted messages on twitter.

When you write about an important occurrence or deal – for example, an increase in ROI, discount coupon or a special promo – you need to highlight it so that readers will take notice.

Always highlight the essential portions of your article by making them bold, italics, by underlining them or by simply changing the color. There are different types of readers. The most common type prefers to skim through the article and only read the highlighted or italicized part (eg. Only the sub-headings or bullets). I am one of them too.

Successful content marketing is all about smart keyword research and identifying your target audience. So, create content that connects to the buying cycle and build a content strategy that will drive the right target audience to the right content.

Take Away This: *A brain uses only 15 watts of power. It cannot focus on everything you write.* **Highlight** *the important portions.*

Chapter 14

ASK FEWER QUESTIONS

Asking fewer or limited questions is the key to conversions. Delete all kinds of unnecessary requests. Do not frustrate your visitors. Too much interrogation or too many forms to fill will act as a repelling force. Less text makes it easier for people to comprehend the message.

Your visitors will simply hit the 'back' button if they encounter too many questions.

We have already covered a portion of this topic in our first chapter, but there's more to it. Visitors are very conscious about the quality, type and quantity of questions that they are asked. Every extra question decreases the chances of form-filling and completion, and in turn, this lowers your conversions. The least interruptive forms with the fewest questions are always the most rewarding. Facebook is the best example of an effective, short and simple sign up form.

Simple always wins over complex. The fewer the form to be filled, the better the conversions. Steve Jobs once said, 'Simpler can be harder than complex. You have to work hard to get your thinking clean to make it simple'.

You should have a simple contact form, and deleting useless questions can directly result in more conversions.

So, keep your forms to only the essentials. Another great example is Dropbox; they only ask what they need. They do not ask for the usernames, security or birth date questions, and nor do they have verification codes.

Let's say you are somebody who sells customized T-shirts. I will show you two approaches to gain your customer's information.

Approach 1:

When a buyer clicks the "Buy" button, you take them to the page where you need their specifications. They need to fill out their preferred shirt color, size, upload image, image size, double sided or single sided, shipping address, number of orders, etc.

Approach 2:

When a buyer clicks the "Buy" button, you take them to the page where they need to choose the size. They will click "Next", and then the page will ask them to select a 'Color'. They will have to click "Next" again, and the page will ask them to upload an image, and so on.

When you create a 'Flow chart' type of a system to process information, the mind doesn't get confused. You will convert a lot more with Approach 2 than with Approach 1

Take Away This: *STOP asking questions when a visitor has pulled out his credit card to buy a product.*

Chapter 15

CONDUCT USABILITY TESTS RAPIDLY

There are numerous things to consider while building a new website. Your site needs to be attractive; it should have the power to engage. It needs to contain all the necessary information that you want to share with your readers. The readers have to find it satisfying, and they should be able to achieve their objectives for which they visited your site.

Usability testing is considered the black horse of increasing conversions. Your site has usability issues if your site is difficult to use or understand. One of the most significant aspects of website building is conducting usability tests. Users can easily figure out how to use a website, and they will immediately understand if a site is unusable. Hence, conducting usability tests is very significant.

Website usability testing enables you to understand all the points of friction. The process is very simple; all you have to do is observe all the users use your site, focus on their experiences and try to locate the patterns. When you have your results, go to your site design to eliminate any obstructions in order to achieve their on-site goals.

Your users view your site differently; they see your site through their eyes and not yours. Usability tests give you direct access to what your users think when they browse your site. You will be able to figure out most of your flaws beforehand, and that is very significant. The crucial goal of any usability test is to figure out whether your users can easily comprehend the given information and whether they can finish the task at hand without any difficulty.

The usability test can be conducted by changing the colour, CTA buttons, images, headlines, or texts. It's often referred to as 'Split testing' or 'A/B Testing'. There are numerous tools and websites, like Unbounce.com, that will help you to create A/B split testing.

I use a site called Usabilityhub (http://fireyourmentor.com/usabilityhub). You can conduct usability tests with real people for free.

You can also do it from your website's dashboard by simply changing the text or images. People who have ignored usability tests are losing more business than they can imagine.

Take Away This: *Make a website for your visitors, not for yourself.*

Chapter 16

DEMONSTRATE YOUR ACCREDITIONS AND ACCOMPLISHMENTS

Demonstrating your accreditations is very crucial. It proves that you are certified. Your accomplishments state that you are not a shady or suspicious character. It helps people realize that you take your business seriously. Your visitors need to be assured that they are in safe hands. It boosts credibility.

There are millions of websites on the internet. More than half of them are either fraud websites or sell a below-average product or service.

Are you really different from them? What makes you different from the rest of them? How will your customers recognize that difference?

Today, social proofs are gaining a lot of popularity. There are many different social media sites, including Facebook, Twitter, Stumble-upon, Instagram, and Tumblr. You can easily integrate testimonials from your social profiles, such as your Facebook page, into your website. There are numerous simple plugins that are freely available in the market. One such example is Getkudos.me

Social proofs help people make decisions faster. It is a very simple psychological phenomenon – 'we determine what's right by what other people think is right'. When people visit a page that has low levels of social media proof, they start thinking of it as less credible. That's because today, social media buttons clog up our screens, so people look at 'shares' and 'likes' as signs of popularity and trustworthiness.

Hence, it is equally important that you remove social proofs from the most noticeable parts of your site, if their counts are low. However, a total lack of social proofs can drastically decrease conversions, because people automatically assume that your company is not trustworthy, is brand new or your products are not used by anyone.

If you have recently worked with a reputed client, ask

them if they are interested in giving a testimonial. If you have sold your product or service to any Fortune 500 company, seek permission to display their logo on your website.

Are you highly educated or have you ever authored a book? If yes, mention this on your website. If you don't tell your customers about your accreditations and accomplishments, their skepticism will never disappear.

I love the way how Neil Patel, founder of Crazyegg & Quickmetrics, promotes himself as a brand. When you visit his landing page (http://fireyourmentor.com/neilpatel), one thing that will catch your eye is "SOCIAL PROOF". Try to implement something similar on your website.

Take Away This: *If you don't tell them about your achievements, they will never know.*

Chapter 17

INCORPORATE A SALES PITCH

A sales pitch changes the tone of your content. It is very instrumental in converting a potential buyer into a customer. Altering the headline should be your first attempt. A persuasive and convincing sales pitch will be very effective in boosting conversions. The sales pitch should be arousing, stimulating and enchanting.

There are several ways of writing good content. It can be an article for a magazine, a book, a blog or a sales page. You need to implement a sales pitch while drafting out your sales copy. If you write it in a magazine style, you won't convert your visitors into customers.

If your headline piques your visitor's interests, you then have to lead your visitors to a psychological commitment, so that they read every word of your content.

Your content should explain to them how that knowledge will take them closer to their desired goal. You have to sell solutions and not services or products; your potential customers are looking for solutions to their problems.

Features are things that describe your product, but benefits are what people enjoy after using your products.

Your sales pitch is all about what kind of customers you are pitching to.

A customer is only interested in knowing what he or she can get out of your product, so address that directly. The golden rule is always to believe in your product; you need to genuinely believe the fact that your product will benefit your customers. If you are naturally confident about your product, then you are more likely to make a lot of sales.

Another important factor for your customers is whether your service or product will save or make them money, so start pitching by mentioning the figures involved. People are not interested in a very drawn-out sales pitch; concisely get to the point of your sale.

One of the main reasons for writing this guide is to teach you how to write for the web. If you look at it, it's different from writing for a magazine or a newspaper.

Once you finish reading this book, you will know a lot more about writing for the web than **99% of the people** on the internet.

There are still some important checkpoints that we can lay down for implementing a substantial sales pitch.
- Discuss the problem
- Show empathy
- Relate to them with an example
- Tell them how you can solve their problem
- Give them proof that it has helped others
- Remove all barriers and doubts

Take Away This: *Writing for the web is different than writing for a newspaper.*

Chapter 18

EMBED AUDIO AND VIDEO INTO YOUR CONTENT

Including audio and video is very instrumental in increasing conversions. Incorporate introductory videos with brief product descriptions, or embed a teleconference or interview.

Research has proved that websites that have an

introductory video on their sales page have increased their conversion rate by **more than 200%.**

You can also introduce yourself with a small audio or video clip that gives your visitors a sense of affiliation. A real human voice introduces familiarity that will boost conversions.

Videos should be frequently used on your landing pages. Videos provide a medium where your visitors can understand the given information with very little effort. A recent study by eyeviewdigital.com showed that using videos on landing pages boosted conversions by 80%.

Also, video increases the total amount of time people stay on your page. If you feature your employees or yourself in the videos, you can further increase the trust factor.

Even a short video about your product helps a lot. You can embed videos that clearly define the benefits and features of your product, because they are like your sales executives in action. To ensure that people do not lose interest while watching them, make sure your videos describe how your product is better than the rest of the products in the market.

People are always short of time. It takes around 5 minutes to read an article, whereas it takes hardly 1 minute to listen to a video presentation. Most people prefer watching a video rather than going through a 2,000-word article. At the same time, people who don't value their time are most likely not going to pull out their credit cards to make payments.

There are tons of sites like Powtoon.com that allow you to create product demos, explainer videos, and introductory videos with just a few clicks. Alternatively, you can also pay a video developer to make it for you. It's a one-time investment that will give you massive results.

Take Away This: *A picture speaks a thousand words, and so does a video.*

Chapter 19

ADD TESTIMONIALS AND OTHER SOCIAL PROOFS

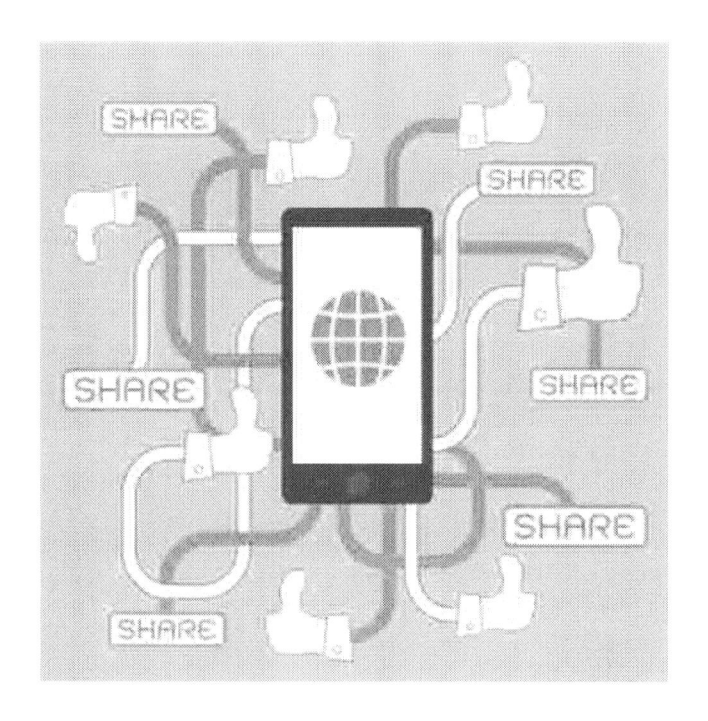

Provide product reviews and testimonials for all your

products. Visitors will be skeptical about your claims, unless you provide social evidence. People are doubtful about big online claims.

Because the personal element of selling is absent, you need to back it up with testimonials and other social proofs. Video testimonials make a very big impact on your visitors. If you can demonstrate how your product has been helpful in solving a problem, it will be very beneficial.

It isn't tough to add a testimonial nowadays. You can either add a plugin from Getkudos.com or simply ask your customers to send you their feedback via email, which you can copy-paste on your site. It's really that simple.

According to Internet Retailer, you can boost conversions by 76% by adding product reviews. Moreover, Jupiter Research stated that 77% of consumers read reviews before purchasing anything online. Product reviews remove doubts from the minds of your potential customers. According to iPerceptions, 63% customers are more likely to convert if the site has product reviews.

Product reviews are more trusted than descriptions made by manufacturers, and in addition to improving conversions, they have many substantial SEO benefits as well. They are another incredible way to add more content, and search engine spiders love unique content that is updated regularly.

Ask your happy customers to write testimonials about their experience. Use their words in your marketing materials. Testimonials build confidence in your products and also foster trust in the eyes of your potential customers.

When visitors surf through your website, they need to know that they are not the only ones contemplating to buy your product or service.

Without some social proof or testimonials, it's impossible to judge the credibility of a good product online, until you have a famous brand. So, until you build a big brand, you need to rely upon social proofs and testimonials to boost sales on your website.

Always embed an image of a client beside his/her testimonial as this fosters credibility.

Take Away This: *If you have something to sell, always include testimonials.*

Chapter 20

CALL TO ACTION

'Call to Action' buttons are the 'Sign Up' buttons or 'Get Started' buttons that you see on a website. Usually, they are located above the fold. They are used for certain elements on a site that ask for an action from the visitor.

It requires some foresight to design CTA buttons into web interfaces. They have to be part of your information process, in order for them to work well.

You have to draw your user's attention with good positioning and by indicating the right size of your call to action buttons.

There are certain things you can consider in order to

increase the Click-Through-Ratio (CTR) to your CTA button. If you simply increase the size of your call to action button, you will exceedingly increment your conversions.

You need to be direct with your customers. Tell your customers what you want, such as, "Try it for free", "Sign up for free", "Add to cart", and so on.

You should also experiment with the color of the CTA button. It should be unique, unconventional and quirky.

For instance, if your website has a blue theme, then the CTA button should be either orange or black. I said orange or black because it will contrast with your blue theme. Make sure that there's no other element in your website with the same color as your CTA button. The logo, the banner, links, the sidebar, and every other element should not be orange or black.

Personalize your CTA buttons and the form. For example, instead of saying "Click Here", you can say, "Get Started" or instead of "Email", try "Your Email". They might look similar to you, but they make a hell of a lot of difference to your conversions. If you can increase your conversions from 1% to 2%, you can easily double your monthly profits.

Example:

You can check out WhatAPortrait.com . They have a CTA button that says "Get Started" on the top right.
Previously, they used to have a smaller CTA button. Once they increased the size of their CTA button by **30%**, they almost **doubled** their CTR (click through rate).

Take Away This: *A website without a CTA button is like a road without signboards.*

Chapter 21

PUBLISH AND UPGRADE FRESH CONTENT FREQUENTLY

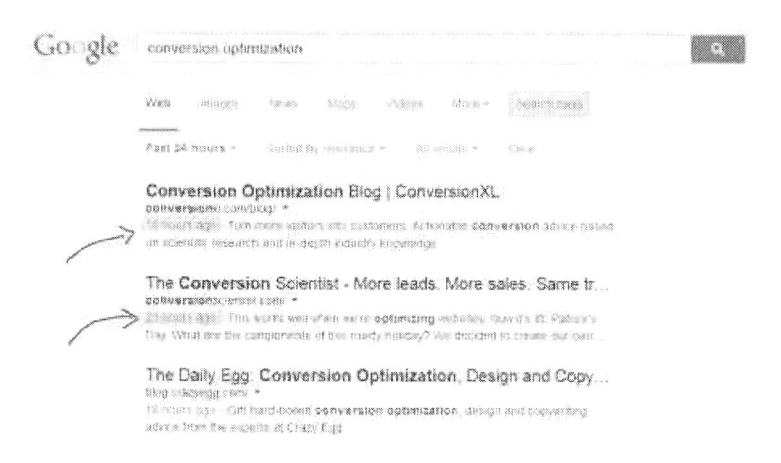

This is a very significant aspect that should not be ignored. Upgrade fresh content regularly. It might seem tedious, but it is very productive. When you enlighten your visitors with fresh new information on a regular basis, they will automatically get hooked to your website, and you will be successful in converting them into customers.

Writing for the web is somewhat different from other

writing platforms. Search trends change every day on Google. If you need a constant source of traffic to your site, you need to regularly update your website with fresh content on the latest trends.

Google Trends can help you find the recent search trends on Google. Alternatively, you can also explore the latest trends on Twitter. There are sites like http://trendsmap.com/ and http://whatthetrend.com/ that can come in handy.

Apart from getting traffic from the latest trends, you also need to understand that Google loves fresh content. They will give your site a higher rank if they find that you are a constant source of fresh content.

Your subscribers will want to see new content on your site. You need to keep in constant touch with your subscribers. If you wait too long to update your blog, you will lose that connection with your subscribers. Your subscribers are priceless; they are your future customers.

You need to take care of their needs and provide them with valuable information with updated articles.

Where Do You Find Fresh Ideas?

I find related long-term keywords in the range of 50-500 'exact monthly searches' using Google keyword Planner (https://adwords.google.com/ko/KeywordPlanner/Home) I will sort around 20-50 such keywords at once.

Then, think of a title for each keyword. Sometimes, I take the help of some free link bait generators (http://fireyourmentor.com/link-bait-generator) available on the internet. I store them in an excel sheet, which I send to my writers on 'hirewriters' (http://fireyourmentor.com/hire-writers). Once I get my articles, I schedule them on my wordpress blog for the next 2-3 months (to publish 1 article every alternate day).

See, it's not really that tough to publish and update your website with fresh articles. 'Outsource' and 'automate' your content writing and publishing work; you will save a lot of time.

Take Away This: *Keep the freshness factor alive.*

Chapter 22

MAKE USE OF BULLET POINTS

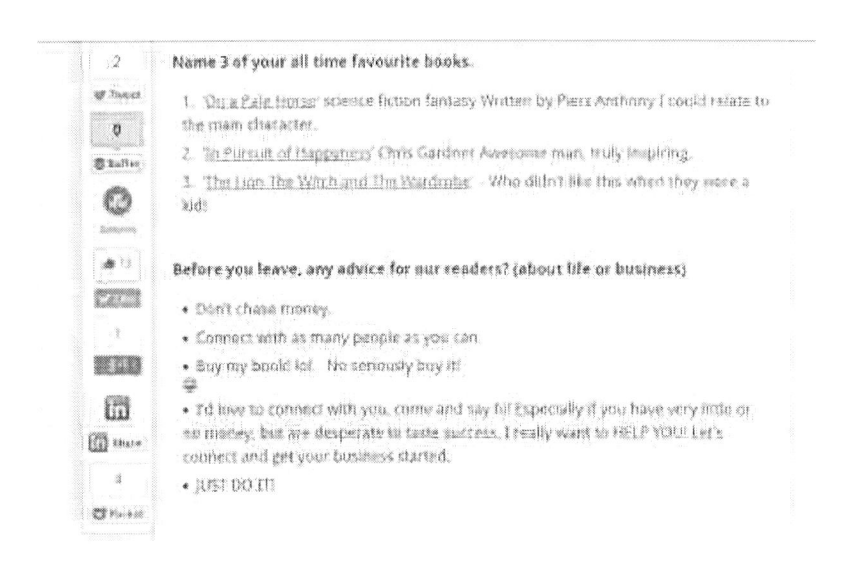

> **Name 3 of your all time favourite books.**
>
> 1. 'On a Pale Horse' science fiction fantasy Written by Piers Anthony I could relate to the main character.
> 2. 'In Pursuit of Happyness' Chris Gardner Awesome man, truly inspiring.
> 3. The Lion, The Witch and The Wardrobe - Who didn't like this when they were a kid?
>
> **Before you leave, any advice for our readers? (about life or business)**
>
> - Don't chase money.
> - Connect with as many people as you can.
> - Buy my book! lol. No seriously buy it!
> - I'd love to connect with you, come and say hi! Especially if you have very little or no money, but are desperate to taste success. I really want to HELP YOU! Let's connect and get your business started.
> - JUST DO IT!

Use bullet points to describe your benefits, offers, terms and conditions. People tend to skim through bullets, graphics, headings, sub-headings, etc.

The majority of your visitors will not thoroughly go through every single line of your content. Normally, online readers tend to simply glance over the information. Hence, make sure that all of your important content is included in bullet points. Bullet points are instrumental in making sales.

As I have already said, "Time is Money" for most people. That's the prime reason they prefer shopping online. You need to understand your target audience. People are time cautious, and no one has the time to go through each and every line of your content.

Using bullets will help you convey your message eloquently. Bullets are instrumental in grabbing your viewer's attention. In real life, one uses a pointer (pen) to control the gaze of the other person. It's body language 101. On the web, we will use bullets instead.

I use bullets for another reason. Bullets put life to your articles. They remove the "boring essay feeling" and replace it with a "great tips feeling".

It's also interesting to see that content that uses bullets are more popular than those without them. Log in to your Google Analytics and check the "time on site" for various articles. You will get to know the difference.

I make it a habit to include bullet points in each and every article that I publish.

Take Away This: *Grab their attention.*

Chapter 23

CONDUCT SPLIT TESTS FREQUENTLY

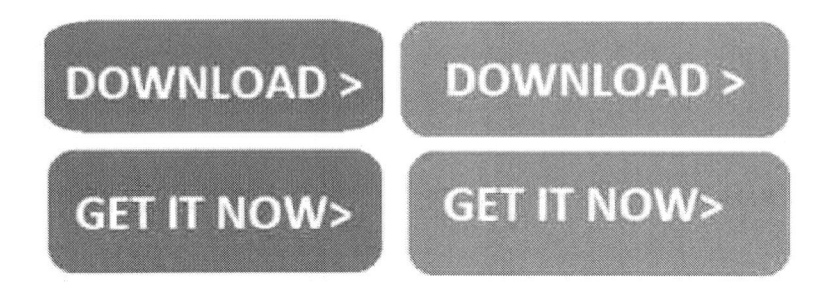

Split tests help owners in understanding what visitors are clicking on or looking at on the website. They can figure out what attracts visitors and what repels them. Through split testing, one can get definite answers about what clicks and what does not.

We have already talked about how important it is to do split testing in Point 14. But the majority of the results depend on how frequently you conduct split testing. I would certainly suggest you to conduct split testing every week.

Sometimes, you run a discount, and sometimes, there's a special occasion. Other times, you offer new products or services. There's no end to split testing. Each and every time you update your website with a new content, you need to split-test it so that you can generate the maximum conversion rates.

It's not the destination; the journey is what matters. Websites are dynamic, and we implement several changes throughout the week. Find a slot on your calendar to do split-testing every now and then. You are likely to double or even triple your profits.

Some people won't take it seriously when I say; you can 'double or triple your profits'. I had a client who sold 'wholesale shoes'. He came to me complaining that only 1 out of 200 people called him back. That's a horrible conversion rate at 0.5%. I checked his website and changed only two things.

1. I personalized the text of his CTA button
2. I changed the color of his CTA button

From then on, he increased his conversion rate from 0.5% to 1%. Now, every 1 out of 100 people who visit his website call him back. He doubled his profit overnight.

Take Away This: *You never know what clicks.*

Chapter 24

EMBED A DEMONSTRATIVE VIDEO

Create and upload a demonstrative video that defines your product's usage clearly. This will improve responses and also create conversions. At times, visitors are clueless about a product's usability; hence, demonstrating it through a video will diminish their skepticism and heighten conversions.

If you have a product that involves some sort of technical

knowledge or mechanical knowledge, you need to create a demonstrative video for each product.

The other day, I brought an 'Elliptical Exercise Bike' from Ebay. It came in around 12 different parts, and I had to assemble it all by myself. Fortunately, I found a demonstrative video on Youtube, uploaded by the manufacturer. It saved my day.

If you want to prevent customer complaints, refunds and dissatisfactions, help the customers fix their problems with a demonstrative video. You can either upload it on your website or your Youtube channel.

As a customer, if I want to buy something that I have not used before, I tend to check a demonstrative video. If I don't find it on the vendor's website, I check it on Youtube.

Sometimes, it's a hassle to go to Youtube and check how the product works. A lot of potential customers will click on 'related videos' and will land on your competitor's website.

You really need to avoid this. Don't let your customers go to Youtube to find a demonstrative video. Have a video right on your site.

Take Away This: *Solve the customer's doubts.*

Chapter 25

CONDUCT A FOLLOW UP

A follow-up will help you in understanding a buyer's perspective. What are their expectations? How do they perceive the product? Or, what are their doubts? You can simply automate the follow-up process and evaluate the results.

There are email softwares like Aweber.com and Mailchimp.com that will help you to schedule your follow-up emails. You can schedule a pre-written format of follow-up emails that will be automatically sent to your subscribers one by one after every few days.

Try not to pitch anything in those follow-up emails. It's better to create a course or tutorial to educate your subscribers. Create a sales funnel that starts with defining a problem, then show empathy and relate to them.

Finally, offer a solution in your last follow-up email.

Whenever you have any free time, try making a series of at least 4-5 follow-up emails for each campaign. Send 1 email per week. With just 4-5 emails, you can easily cover the whole month.

I did a follow-up campaign a few days ago for one of my products, and it helped me triple my revenue that was solely generated from my sales page. Selling your products or services via a follow-up email works because you build a relation with your subscribers.

A follow-up can also be a reminder. It's very easy to forget about a website you visited 4 days ago. One needs a constant reminder that says, "I am alive".

A follow-up is necessary to keep in touch with your loyal subscribers. It's like talking to your friends every now and then. Sometimes, you invite them over for dinner, or you simply leave a message.

Take Away This: *Stay in touch.*

Chapter 26

DON'T OFFER DISCOUNTS

People are fascinated by bargains; hence, never showcase discounted product prices on your website. When you publicize your discounted prices and change them from time to time, people won't buy your product without a discounted price.

This is true not only for online buyers but for offline

buyers as well. People always expect to get a discounted price. If they don't get it, they will look for it elsewhere.

If you want to run a promo offer, try offering something complementary rather than reducing your price. Try to over-sell by offering combo-offers. It works better than offering straight discounts on the MRP.

Think of a website that you know that offers huge discounts. Think of yourself as a customer. Will you buy a product from that store if it doesn't run a discount? There's a bigger chance that you will drop the idea to buy 'right now' and wait until they run another promo.

Take Away This: *Discounts suck.*

Chapter 27

EVALUATE WEBSITE METRICS

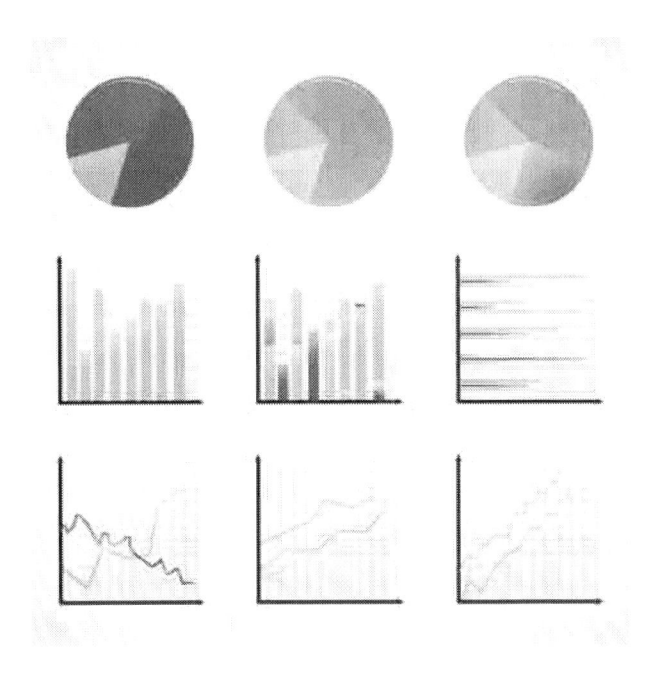

Assess your website metrics. Evaluate how your conversion rates tally with other website metrics. Calculate the changes that are being induced by other metrics.

Here are some examples of 'other' metrics, such as:

- Bounce Rate
- Time spent on the site
- Time spent on individual pages
- Social shares
- Comments
- Links and mentions
- Sign ups

You need to always re-evaluate these metrics by comparing them with the other pages of your website.

If a particular article gets 300% more shares than the rest, try to find the reason behind it. A constant look at these metrics will help you analyze what works better for your audience and how you can convert them better.

Keep a tab on it and store it in an excel sheet. It's fine if you do it just once every month. Google Analytics (http://www.google.com/analytics/), Getclicky (http://fireyourmentor.com/getclicky), Crazyegg.com are some of the tools that you can use to help you evaluate these metrics.

Site owners don't care much about things like bounce rates, time spent on site, and comments, because these elements can vary from industry to industry. However, you need to analyze them and find out what suits your audience.

If a particular article receives 30 comments, while your average comments per article is just 5, try to find the reason behind it. You must have done something differently with this article, since it has engaged so many of your readers. Once you identify what works best, you can implement similar ideas in the rest of your articles.

These changes will take time and won't happen overnight.

Take Away This: *Find the magic potion.*

Chapter 28

LIMIT THE CLICKS BETWEEN THE SALES PAGE AND THE ORDER PAGE

Most of your visitors are restless and impatient. They are short of time and get bored easily. Simplify your check-out process. It will increase your conversion rates. Limit the clicks that lead your visitors to the order page.

There are many websites that require registration before buying a product. It's the wrong approach. They lose more customers than they can imagine.

THIS IS IMPORTANT:

In 2014, the latest trend in website designing is to bring everything under 1 page.

It doesn't mean that the whole website has just 1 page. There are number of pages, like a blog, but they are not targeted well. When a customer lands on your website, he should see the landing page with the following features:

- Social Proof
- About Us
- Pricing
- Buy Now Button.

Some examples of such sites are:

1. www.munmi.org (my company's site)
2. www.restaurantengine.com (random site)
3. www.bounceexchange.com (random site)

Your sales process will become futile if you add too many pages between the sales page and the order page. If your visitors can reach the order page quickly, your conversions will definitely increase.

Whenever a buyer clicks on the 'Buy Now' button, it should directly take him to the 'Check Out' page. Very often, people tend to create a wide bridge between the 'sales page' and the 'check out' page by adding extra pages like discounts, contact info, and so on. Remove such unnecessary pages.

It's often noticed that people **lose around 20% of their**

buyers when they create a bridge between their 'sales page' and their 'check out' page.

Take Away This: *Take the shortcut.*

Chapter 29

UNCLUTTER YOUR HOME PAGE

Firstly, understand the type of website you have. Is it a blog where you want people to read different articles, or is it a website through which you are trying to sell a product or a service?

If you have a blog, you can elevate it to 'magazine style' by using one of the magazine style themes from theme forest.

(http://www.fireyourmentor.com/go/magazinethemes)

However, if you have a website through which you are trying to sell something, you better unclutter your homepage. It's been proved that when one removes everything from the homepage (including the sidebar) and only maintains a simple sales page, conversion rate increases by more than 200%.

Do not confuse your readers with too many actions on the homepage. They will become uninterested and bounce off the page. If you want to bring your work and endeavors into the limelight and foster your visitor's attention, then clear and categorize your homepage. Simply focus on or highlight a single, distinct and definite action.

There are numerous websites that are trying to expand their businesses online. Most of them try to put every single little detail on their homepage. It creates more confusion than clarity.

Let's say, if you have a "About us" page, why would you want to have the blog posts displayed in the sidebar? You have brought your visitors to the "About us" page to know you better, to show your accomplishments, to help them trust and recognize your work. There's no point in showing them the last few updates your company has made or the 10 latest articles from your blog.

Just think about it from a customer's perspective. "Show them what they want to see, not what you want to show them".

Take Away This: *Be clean and tidy.*

Chapter 30

BACK UP YOUR CLAIMS WITH PROOFS

Do you make enough claims to your visitors? How do you think they will trust you? There are around 90% people scamming each other on internet sites. Websites have become more and more insecure. You better back up your claims with some solid proof.

Your visitors do not know you; hence, they do not trust

you. The only way you can convince them is by displaying facts, testimonials, videos, audios, demonstrations, user reviews and feedbacks. Present social proofs such as charts, checks, and endorsements. Back up all your claims with proofs, and make them persuasive and convincing.

If you are promoting an app via your website, show how many downloads and reviews this app or your previous app has received. If you are an author, show them how your previous books have performed. If you sell softwares, then show them how this software has helped others.

It gets even easier when you are an affiliate. Say you are an amazon.com affiliate. You can select a product, and along with it, you can showcase all the positive reviews it has received from all the buyers.

Ramit Sethi, an American Personal Finance advisor and Bestselling Author does it flawlessly with his blog (http://fireyourmentor.com/ramit). He has numerous social proofs on his websites. No one will ever doubt his credibility.

All you need is to display some social proof to your visitors, so that they can trust you effortlessly.

Take Away This: Be a "superman".

Chapter 31

ACCELERATE YOUR SHIPPING PROCESS

If you provide services, let me enlighten you with a secret that will help you grow your income. **"ACCELERATE YOUR DELIVERY PROCESS"**.

That's the most lucrative secret that many Fortune 1000 companies use to augment their reputation, so that they can quickly gain more customers.

Expedite your shipping and transportation processes. Try to provide next-day shipping of products if possible; it will boost conversions. Customers become very happy and satisfied when they get instant deliveries. They talk about it and spread the word around.

Check out some feedbacks of certain power sellers on Ebay. Most of their positive feedbacks revolve around their fast delivery process. It makes customers eager to order from them again.

BUY NOW >
Delivery within 48 hrs.

While drafting a web copy, you should let your visitors know that you offer **"Super Sonic Delivery"**. How will you do it? Well, it's easy. Just insert a small banner in the sidebar or simply put a text below the 'Buy Now' button.

If you have read books on marketing, you will often find that authors have mentioned this tactic as the single most effective technique for service providers.

It can give you a competitive advantage or can also help you with market penetration (without taking the 'price' factor into consideration).

If you are a new service provider in the market, you can grab attention by providing the best 'delivery time'.

I started providing SEO services in Wickedfire forums back in 2010-11. I used this very technique to quickly grab attention and establish myself as a respected seller among a ton of quality SEO providers. I received over 500 positive feedbacks (100%) within a span of 1-2 years.

I received most of these reviews because I used to submit them their reports within 4-5 hrs. Now, I don't even provide reports to 'save time'. People still buy from me because I have already built that reputation in front of my customers.

Take Away This: *'The fast and the furious' wins the race.*

Chapter 32

GET TO THE BOTTOMLINE FAST

Occasionally, getting to the point quickly or even deleting certain paragraphs stimulates conversions. Be straightforward, rather than beating around the bush. Test by deleting the first few paragraphs and relish the results.

Keep on split testing. This time, I will ask you to split test with texts. Try to come up with the fastest way to impress your visitors and turn them into customers.

The other day, I was speaking to a sales representative because I was interested in buying a tablet. I kept asking him the difference between a Samsung Galaxy tab and an iPad. He kept replying that they both have the same specifications, except for their operating systems. Each time I asked him whether I should go for an iPad or a Samsung Galaxy Tab, I got the same reply. Ultimately, I couldn't make my decision and returned back home. The next day, I visited an online shopping site, compared the specifications of each tablet side-by-side and I purchased it online.

The point I am trying to make is, don't confuse your buyers. Get to the bottom line fast. Even if you know that 2 products are almost similar, try to find their unique selling proposition (USP). If there is nothing to differentiate them, try segregating them based on their color, size, shape etc. That's what Apple has done with their latest iPhone 5C. Smart, isn't it?

Let's take an example of a site that sells baby care products.

People who visit this site will mostly have 1 query in common. "Will this product be appropriate for my baby's age-group?"

When you know the common query, try to solve it by getting to the bottom-line fast. Amazon.com has done it brilliantly with their "Children's Book" section. Check it out.

Take Away This: *Don't beat around the bush.*

Chapter 33

ACCOMODATE A FREE TRAIL BUTTON

People are drawn by free stuff. Embed a 'Free Trial' button and experience the results yourself. The 'Free Trial' button is more effective in boosting conversions than the 'Buy Now' button.

Your main goal is to convert your visitors into customers.

People are often uncertain about making a purchase. Try to overcome that hurdle by offering them a trial copy of your product or service.

You can either provide a free trial or a discounted trial copy for a few days. Some people offer it for 5 days, and others for 30 days. It depends on the type of product or service you are selling. A wise decision would be to search for your competitors and study what they are offering.

People are 10 times more likely to sign up for a free trial rather than making a direct purchase. **More than 30%** of your trial users will end up buying your product or service (provided it's a great product with great value).

It's a much better conversion rate if you compare it with people who would directly buy your product or service.
SAAS (software as a service) companies like moz.com and serps.com use this technique to get tons of sign-ups.
However, there are a lot of people who are looking for freebies and will never sign up as your customer. Beware of such people.

Will you buy a product that's available for free?

Absolutely not! Nobody will pay for something that's available for free. You need to bind them into some contract that says, *try this and then buy. If you are unhappy with our product, then don't use it. But, don't come looking for freebies.*

In order to avoid the segment that will never pay and prevent them from wasting your resources, ask them to fill their Credit Card details to use your "Free Trial". Once the trial period is over, it will auto-rebill. The conversion might be less than usual but, you will at least get quality leads.

Take Away This: *Try and then buy.*

Chapter 34

OFFER PRODUCT IMAGES

Most people are insecure about buying products online. They feel vulnerable and unsafe because everything is virtual.

Hence, offering product images fosters and enforces the credibility and trustworthiness of the seller. It enlightens a potential customer about the existence of the particular product. Their skepticism is put to rest, and this directly leads to increased conversions.

Let me give you an example:

Will you ever buy a handbag that says leather strips, adjustable straps, sturdy handle, red color, medium size and 3 separate chambers, without any actual picture of the handbag?

When people shop online, they cannot touch a product physically. So, you need to offer an image of the product, which will visually satisfy them.

For example, assume that you are selling software or an ebook. They are not tangible. So to persuade your potential customers, you need to have an image of your product. You can't convert a visitor into a buyer without showing him or her a picture of the product.

A powerful image speaks for itself. Words may be very crucial, but in many instances, a persuasive visual component is a mandatory part of the selling process.

Leveraging product images can provide a significant boost in your conversion rates.

Why do you think Amazon asks Kindle authors to get a book cover of 1000 pixels or more?

The reason is quite simple. Kindle books are intangible. You can't touch them. Even though it's virtual, a quality book cover will force a customer to view kindle books as any other normal paperback book.

Take Away This: *You believe what you see.*

Chapter 35

ALWAYS OFFER EXTENSIVE GUARANTEES

Would you every buy a product that offers no guarantee? Not even for 30 days?

Personally, I wouldn't. We as consumers want some sort of assurance when we spend our heard-earned money.

According to a study, products that offer extended

guarantees are often most likely to be trusted as a brand. You are sending a message that the product will be in good condition, even after the guarantee is over.

Take risks by offering extensive (full) guarantees. Most of your potential buyers refrain from buying your product, even if your product is all they need. Providing guarantees is an excellent idea because it provides solace to your customers. It allows your customers to realize that you will help them if the product does not match their expectations.

Offering guarantees lowers the risks in your customer's mind. It enables them to understand that you trust your services or products. This simplifies their decision-making process. People are hesitant to offer guarantees for various reasons. Most of them are concerned that they will get many refund requests and are unsure about what guarantees to offer.

If you are getting too many refund requests, chances are you are doing something wrong. Overpricing your product or service, selling to a market that is unfit for your service or product, poor quality product or service – these are several factors that may be generating refund requests.

There are situations when you are unable to offer a guarantee for more than 30 days. In that case, offer an extended guarantee for 6 months or a year by charging a little extra from your customers.

Extended guarantees stimulate people to buy your product, even if they do not avail the guarantee. If you offer a simple-to-comprehend guarantee that lowers the buyer's risk, your customer will certainly feel secure about his investment.

Take Away This: *Customers need assurance.*

Chapter 36

PROMOTE LIST BUILDING

It's an art to capture visitors. Nobody would give you their email address to send them promotional offers. Most people do it wrong when it comes to capturing email addresses.

Here are a few things you need to remember:

1. Exit pop-up performs 300-500% better than entry pop-ups.
2. Offer them something valuable and exclusive to capture their email address.
3. Bigger opt-in forms, bigger CTA buttons, bigger

headlines perform better.
4. Always offer something for FREE. Don't forget to highlight the word, "FREE" in your opt-in form.

Try to build your list by accumulating opt-in emails and follow up with this list from time to time. Collecting email addresses and other contact information is crucial for augmenting your conversion rates.

You can expect higher responses to your promotions if you are successful in generating your customer's physical address and number. On their first visit, more than 90% of your visitors won't buy anything. They are either still in the research phase or simply browsing. It takes effort, time and persistence to build a relationship and instill confidence.

So, when you already know that the overwhelming majority won't buy anything, there's no point in pushing it. You are just going to drive them away. Instead, focus on capturing their email addresses and start building a trusting relationship. We have already discussed about sales funnel and conducting follow-ups. You can accomplish all these if you have a good list.

A good list is an asset. Say it's Christmas, and you want to run a special promo. If you have a good list of subscribers, you can easily send an email to all of them with the coupon codes. You can make tons of sales overnight.

"Build it, nurture it, and preserve it".

List building should be your top priority if you are new to internet marketing. Almost every successful marketer will tell you 'money is in the list'. Building a list isn't the only important thing; creating a 'warm list' is what's essential.

There are mainly two types of lists, 'cold list' and 'warm list'. The list of subscribers who have not been contacted over a very long time is called a cold list. Obviously, their response to your emails will be low. As for a warm list, the owner stays in regular touch with the subscribers, communicating with them and giving them a solid reason to stay subscribed. Creating a warm list is very essential, because it means that any call to action that you send will get a better response, thereby increasing your conversion rates.

What softwares to use?
You can use email marketing software like Aweber (http://www.fireyourmentor.com/go/aweber), Mailchimp or Getresponse.

Since I use wordpress, I use Wp lead magnet plugin (http://www.fireyourmentor.com/go/wpleadmagnet) for "Exit pop-ups". If you use a different platform, you might need to get a custom plugin from your developer.

Take Away This: *A good list is an asset.*

Chapter 37

INTEGRATE RED HYPERLINKS

Red is the color of 'Power' and 'Passion'. People use red wrappers for gifts. The color red has a very dynamic connotation; it makes a person think of something covetable, desirable and appealing.

Research has proved that red links convert the best, as it is the natural color of most links used online. Click-through rates are boosted by making links red. Beamax, a Belgium-based company that manufactures and distributes projection screens for meeting rooms and home cinemas, boosted their click-through rate by making their links red.

In terms of design, red seizes attention and can be used to communicate many emotions. It shouts out from the page and it's undoubtedly popular in logo designs; examples include the logos of CocaCola, Colgate, Youtube, Canon, and CNN. Red is associated with strength, power and determination.

It is a very emotionally intense color. Red has a very high visibility, and that's why fire equipment, stop signs and stop lights are painted red. It is frequently featured in national flags, and it brings images and texts to the forefront. It can be used to motivate people to make decisions; hence, it is the most suitable color for the 'Buy Now' and 'Click Here' buttons. It is a very intense color and should be used intelligently in your designs.

Blue Hyperlinks are very common and are almost everywhere, from Google to Bing. When you use red hyperlinks on your website, people will believe that it will take them to a 'different page'. The special page hidden under that 'red hyperlink' can generate a lot of curiosity and inquisitiveness.

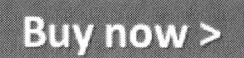

[Buy now >] OR [Buy now >]

A sense of affiliation comes with a red hyperlink. Interestingly, a red **'Buy Now'** button converts better than any other color.

Color has a huge impact on human behavior. Any CTA button should stand out from the rest of the page, so if you have a blue, white or grey design, you should change it to red so that it attracts attention. People tend to click on things that stand out.

Take Away This: *Red is powerful.*

Chapter 38

OFFER GIVEAWAYS

Giving away materials for free can establish your trustworthiness and the quality of your products to all your potential customers.

When your potential customers experience the quality that you deliver for the free product, they will be more than willing to explore your other products.

There's nothing like a good giveaway to make people talk about your products and business. Giveaways are another great alternative to boost your email subscriptions.

Within a very short time, you can easily triple your email list by offering amazing stuff to your visitors. Giveaways need a bit of investment and proper research of what exactly your audience wants.

Many reputed marketing organizations like Marketing Sherpa, Wildfire, Social Media Examiner, have created many case studies to demonstrate the effectiveness of giveaways from increasing sales and traffic to creating massive brand awareness.

As long as you have a valuable prize to give, your visitors will take any action that you want them to take.

Three examples of excellent giveaways are mentioned below:

Coupon Codes:

People love discounts on everything that they purchase. For years, marketers have used coupon codes to lure visitors to make a purchase.

Free Whitepapers or Ebooks:

Giving away a free Whitepaper or Ebook in exchange for a user's email address is a very common and widely used conversion optimization technique. If the Ebook or Whitepaper has valuable information, then the user is more willing to provide their contact information.

Free Consultation or Advice:

All consumers seek expert advice while deciding on making a particular purchase. A conversion technique that many famous companies use is offering free advice or consultation on their service or product if the users reach out and contact the company through their official website.

If you can find the right sponsors, then investment may never be a problem. If you give stuff away for free, you will secure massive conversion benefits. The greater the giveaway, the better the chances are for conversions. So, make sure you utilize your giveaway potential.

When you are offering a giveaway, you need to have a proper sales funnel.

Firstly, you need to capture their email address.

Secondly, try to get their feedback or review on your social media pages and use it as a social proof to sell your products to your future customers.

You can up-sell your original products to those who have already grabbed a giveaway. Moreover, you can use them to help you promote your products by liking your FB page or tweeting about it. The possibilities are endless.

You just need to figure out what works best for you. Devote some time to create a winning strategy to giveaway some products for promoting your brand.

There are tons of authors on amazon.com who uses the very same technique to drive sales for their paid books.

Take Away This: *People love giveaways.*

Chapter 39

EMBED YOUR PHONE NUMBER INTO THE HOMEPAGE

Adding a phone number to your website enhances your credibility, thereby boosting conversions. The company "LessAccounting" witnessed a **1.8% growth** in conversions after adding a phone number on their site.

Having a visible phone number on the home page

enhances the trust factor and therefore increases the sign-ups too. Having a phone number brings peace of mind to customers and people you do business with. At the very least, it removes any 'fly-by-night-operation' fear that they may have.

Around **10-20% people** will drop from the 'check out' page because they will have some unanswered doubts and queries. If you don't have a phone number that they can call and get their doubts clarified or questions answered, you will lose these potential customers forever.

A study conducted by Chantily, indicated that 75% of small business sites do not have an email link or phone number on their homepage. Your site should have a phone number and a very clear email link on the homepage. If you also have a physical location, add the full address with the zip code and map directions as well.

Adding your phone number and also a local street address is a good signal to the search engines. Make sure that it is in the text and not in an image. It's great for search engine bots, and it is also helpful for people who browse from their mobile phones, as your number will be clickable.

Take Away This: *You need to post a phone number on every page of your website.*

Chapter 40

ADD CONTEXT TO ALL YOUR PRODUCTS

Basically, context means showcasing real life examples of your product in action. The more you demonstrate the product in real life, the easier it gets for a potential customer to decide that this is what they actually want to buy.

If you are offering a physical product, then do everything you possibly can to make it look real. Take photos of it from all angles and with a person, and come out with other ways to make your product look real.

The other night, I ordered a video game. The site that offered the lowest price had no specifications about the game. I checked 2-3 sites to find out the minimum system requirements. Fortunately, I came back to the site to buy the game after doing my research, but most customers will never return.

Buyers want to know whether a product is compatible with the other products they own, and they also want to view the added accessories that come with a product. If you do not provide the necessary information, they will go to your competitor's site or to your manufacturer's site to find out the information.

When you look at extremely famous companies, like Amazon.com, you will find it amazing how much detail they put in to product descriptions. They not only have descriptions listed by the manufacturers, but they also have descriptions provided by expert reviews. Very often, you will get to see multiple product photos, product dimensions, related products and product reviews. These details give the customer an idea of what they will be buying before hitting the Add To Cart Button.

You need to have enough content in the description field when you list a product. You should try and answer each and every possible question a customer might have. A buyer often goes through comparing specifications between different products. In that case, you need to pitch how a product is better than another one. Give a clear-cut answer so that it helps the customer make a purchasing decision quickly and easily.

Take Away This: *Describe your products completely.*

Chapter 41

OFFER PREMIUM OPTIONS

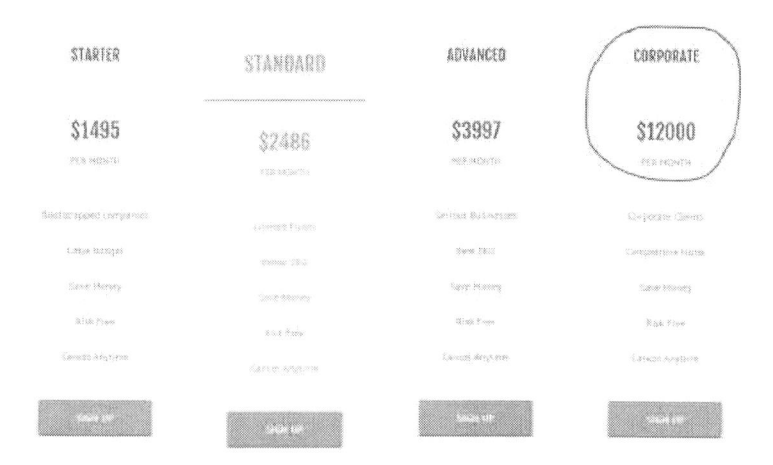

Customers have different financial needs. Some customers may be looking for the best that money can buy, and others may be looking for a bargain. Therefore, premium options can ensure that different customers pay for what they want. This ultimately helps in increasing conversions. Offering varied groups of products and services ensures that each group of customers pays for what they want to buy.

It is important to remember that *80% of your income comes from 20% of your buyers*. Don't believe me? Check your sales history and analyze how much revenue you have earned from your biggest clients and customers.

The **20%** buyers are premium buyers who will pay big for the value. So, instead of focusing on the **80%** odd audience, focus on this hyperactive **20%** and offer them premium rates. You will sky rocket your profits if you do it the right way.

When you list the price on your website, make a package, keeping these hyperactive buyers in mind. If you are selling books on Kindle, then create a Combo offer for 10x the price. You will still make sales from premium buyers.

I offer SEO and Internet marketing services to my clients. I have ensured that I create a corporate package that's at least 10x the price of the basic package. I know that I won't make many sales from this package, but the 1 or 2 sales that I will make will make all the difference. You will get a clear idea when you check out my pricing page: http://munmi.org/#pricing

Take Away This: *There're always some premium customers who will pay BIG.*

Chapter 42

SIMPLIFY YOUR CHECKOUT PROCESS

Your check-out process might seem secure to you, but if the process involves too many steps or requires too much information, chances are, most of your customers will change their minds. One of the many ways to increase your conversions is by simplifying your check-out process. Most customers are more likely to make a purchase if they don't have to go through the hassle of signing up or registering.

Try to consolidate your entire check-out flow into one or two pages. The fewer the clicks, the lesser the people drop out of the flow. Try to eliminate all unwanted questions from your check-out process. Ask for information only pertaining to the purchase, such as shipping address or billing. Try to skip all the unnecessary questions such as "where did you come from" or "where are you going".

Optimizing the check-out process improves revenues and also gives a better experience to customers. Most people drop their purchases while on the check-out page. People appreciate simplicity while carrying out transactions online. By simply tweaking a few details in your check-out process, you can easily increase conversions. Optimize and test the check-out process to make sure that you are getting good revenues.

Avoid trivial design elements that interfere with the check-out process. Perform A/B testing of numerous check-out designs to figure out which ones converts the best. Showing customers what to expect in the check-out process is a good idea. Customers should have an idea of the kind of information required in the next stage, and they should be informed that they can easily review their order during the check-out process.

If possible, eliminate all distractions, like the sidebar or the menu bar. Enable the customer to see only his order information and the check-out button. Try to grab their focus and interest on completing the purchase. If you let their eyes wander, you will lose many potential customers who will eventually click something else and move away from *your 'check-out' page*.

Take Away This: *Don't distract a customer who is ready to buy.*

Chapter 43

PROVIDE LIVE SUPPORT

Hire operators to interact with your potential customers by running a live support button on your site. Conversions increase when live operators clarify visitor's doubts right away. If used correctly, the live chat option can increase conversion rates by giving customers immediate access to a support agent or operator while they are still on your site.

Very often with major purchases, the customers take time to think about it. Generally they want to compare different models and prices to determine if they are getting a good deal. The live chat customer support can identify customers who have spent longer time on certain pages and have been comparing different brands. The live chat support option is not just about answering questions and clarifying queries, if used correctly it can boost conversions rapidly.

The finest live chat softwares comprise of intelligent analytics that can be used to study exactly which pages the customers are visiting, how long they spend on those pages and how exactly they got there. Virgin Airlines has not only used the live chat option to sell more tickets, but they mostly use it to up-sell customers. Virgin Airlines has created enormous conversion rates by up-selling their customers as they finish their orders.

The order value from users who use the live chat option is 15% more than the ones who don't. Moreover the visitors who engage in live chat tend to convert 3.5 times as often as the ones who don't. Live chat is much cheaper than phone calls or emails because one single live chat agent can do the work of around 17 customer care executives who handle calls or emails.

We have already discussed about how Zopim.com can help you to set up a live chat plugin on your website on Point 8.

Take Away This: Be available 24x7 for your customers.

Chapter 44

INCLUDE CUSTOMER PHOTOS ON YOUR HOMEPAGE

Including customer photos and testimonials that accompany the photos can increase your conversion rates by leaps and bounds. Customer photos make a site vibrant and they also make it convert better. People are no longer interested in simple browsing; they want to experience the site.

Using the right photos can get you to connect better with your audience and also boost your site's conversions. Most customers buy for emotional reasons, so if you make them feel just right, they might take action. Be careful in choosing the images for your site; a positive image generates positive emotions. It could be a smirk, a gesture or a simple smile.

Using real human images can get your visitors to focus more and draw them to a common cause. The sites that don't have a celebrity brand should consider using staff or customers' photos.

A recent study conducted by a professor at **Simon Fraser University** found that sites that used 'friendly faces' were recognized as more trustworthy and appealing compared to those that didn't. Adding pictures of smiling human faces gives off positive and happy vibes and also results in more visitors taking action. You also have to consider the effect of showing a male face to a female or a young face to an older crowd.

A recent landing page test conducted by Wider Funnel revealed that 18.2% people are more likely to convert if real human images rather than thumbnails of art pieces are shown. Images of people can produce very strong positive or negative reactions; they can either repel or persuade.

Take Away This: *Prove that real people have already brought your product and are happy with their purchase.*

Chapter 45

MAKE USE OF GOOGLE OPTIMIZER

Google optimizer is a mind-blowing tool that enables you to escalate the value of your current sites and traffic without spending any money. Google Optimizer tests and optimizes site design and content. With the help of this tool, you can easily and quickly increase your ROI and revenue. The Google optimizer is a free tool, so if you have budgetary concerns, know that you don't have to spend any money to start testing.

The Google optimizer is best for people who run SEO or PPC campaigns to drive traffic to landing pages for conversions. The ultimate goal of the Google optimizer is to get you as many conversions as possible considering your cost per acquisition goals.

With Google website optimizer, you can set a maximum cost per acquisition, which is the maximum amount that you are willing to pay for a conversion, or a target cost per acquisition, which is the amount that you are willing to pay for a conversion.

On average, sites that use the conversion optimizer increase their conversions by approximately 21%.

You don't have to be a web developer to use this tool effectively; setting up an experiment in the Google optimizer is very easy. It creates very dynamic and extremely high-converting pages, and it uses Google analytics for its tracking purposes. It uses both A/B split and multivariate testing.

A good looking website doesn't mean that it will sell products or services or draw traffic instantly. Many more factors are involved, other than design, and that's where the Google Optimizer comes in. Leveraging a free tool that helps you to accelerate your sales is about as good as it gets.

Take Away This: *Make use of this free tool.*

Chapter 46

INCLUDE POP-UP & SIGN-UP FORMS

Pop-ups are known to increase email subscriptions. Many companies have suggested that a pop-up sign-up form aided in boosting conversion rates. Some people seem to hate pop-ups, but the truth is, they can double your conversion rates. You can also give the hellobar.com a shot; it's like the gateway drug of pop-ups.

Pop-ups generate a lot of controversy. They can be infuriating but they are also exceedingly high-converting. A web page with a pop-up will see much more conversions than the same page without the pop-up. Remember to add a well-designed pop-up because it converts much better than a poorly crafted one. Your pop-up must provide the information that the reader believes is worth his or her time.

A study conducted by the MACLABS research team showed that using a simple pop-up on the landing page increases account sign-ups by 63%. If you want to avoid a hideous pop-up that chases your audience away, avoid the drawbacks mentioned below:

- Your visitors feel tricked if your pop-up has a hidden or inactive exit button.
- Pushy pop-ups accumulate customers who are uninterested and rarely convert into paying

customers.
- Massive pop-ups compel people to leave.
- The pop-ups that are designed to look like browser dialog boxes are deceitful.
- Multiple pop-ups look like 'spam' and are deeply mistrusted.

Getting all the elements right isn't only about balancing 'bad user experience' with 'great conversion rates'. You have to create a win-win scenario in which an enjoyable user experience reinforces an increase in conversion rates.

My suggestion would be to use an "Exit Pop-up". It's not irritating to your visitors, and at the same time, you put that pop-up right in their face. I highly recommend 'Wpleadmagnet' as it can track mouse movements of your visitors and knows when to show an exit pop-up. (http://www.fireyourmentor.com/go/wpleadmagnet)

Take Away This: *Don't forego a chance to capture emails.*

Chapter 47

INVOKE THE HUMAN EMOTION

Human beings are emotional creatures. We act off emotion rather than simple logic. Emotion is often controlled by people who are trying to sell to us. For instance, the perfume industry sold $30.5 billion worth of products in 2006. Logically, perfumes contain all kinds of harmful chemicals placed into fine-shaped bottles, designed to make all of us smell better. Human beings tend to purchase based on emotion, and smelling good makes us feel better. Hence, emphasizing the emotional benefits of your product or service can automatically increase your sales.

Of course hard facts are useful, but make sure you wrap them up in a way that puts emphasis on emotion. Your prospects and customers are not stupid; they understand what you are trying to convey. So, make them feel happy and wanted, and they will connect with you better. Leveraging emotions can be very useful, but how you do it is what matters.

Most of our decisions are based on emotions. Our emotions guide us and help us in making our decisions. You have to understand how your product makes people feel and what kind of emotions it generates.

Once you have figured that out, use these emotions to lead your visitors into action with your design. You have to use colors to persuade people into feeling some sort of emotion towards your product. Certain colors make us feel sad, happy, annoyed, inspired, excited and much more.

You can always make all the changes you want, but if you are not following the emotional journey of your visitors, you are leaving a lot of money on the table.

Emotions are very powerful; for example, you may not remember the exact story of a movie, but you might still remember whether you enjoyed it, loved it or hated it. It is hard to change an evaluation that is formed on the basis of an emotion. We begin to comprehend it as 'valid' and 'true', which makes it our reality.

Take Away This: *Leverage emotions.*

Chapter 48

BRUSH UP YOUR COPYWRITING SKILLS

The skill of copywriting should be mastered by all online business owners. Be it writing sales letters or PPC ads, copywriting is one of the most significant techniques that will help you to increase conversions. Most business owners spend lots of time studying SEO strategies and PPC marketing tactics. However, devoting some time to learn the skill of copywriting can be very advantageous.

Having the ability to persuade others through your words is a priceless skill that is useful in all aspects of life. As your copywriting knowledge enhances, you will be capable of improving your pages and witness increased conversions. Mastering copywriting is like having the potential to print money. Leading copywriters easily make over $1 million per year for writing sales campaigns. You will miss out big time if you do not put in the effort to master copywriting. Apple Inc and many other big brands in the world use copywriting to their advantage.

The aim of a regular piece of content is to inform people, but the purpose of a web copy is to make people take action. Hiring a good professional copywriter can be expensive; hence, mastering this skill can be very useful. You don't need to be an excellent writer to create a good web copy; you just need to adhere to the right process and instill certain key principles about writing content that converts.

Here are the six principles for writing conversion-boosting content:

✓ Conduct in-depth research on the customers, product or service, and the competition. This can be time-intensive, but it can be very beneficial.

✓ Write the outline of your copy first. It takes only a few minutes to write an outline that can provide a road map for the entire project.

✓ Avoid jargons, be specific and make the copy about your customers and not all about you and your product or service. If your copy is all about you and not about your potential customers, you won't make much of an impact.

✓   Once your content is ready, give it a conversion boost. Check if your value proposition is clear and understandable. You can make a list of all the possible questions that your visitors might have, especially during the buying process, and address them.

✓   Revise your content and take a fresh look at it the next day to spot errors, inconsistencies and flaws. Get some people to read your copy before you publish it, and ask them to give you their feedback.

✓   Testing your copy is very crucial because there is no way to predict how your copy will perform. Sometimes, your value proposition may be weak or your offer doesn't match the audience's demand. Begin with A/B testing value propositions.

Nowadays, online media is the most reliable source of information, and copywriting is rapidly gaining importance in today's world.

In earlier times, selling products through the electronic or print media was the only way to reach a maximum number of audiences. Now, online media offers a much better source of information than the two aforementioned mediums. You never get a second chance to make a good impression, and the only way to accomplish it is by having convincing content on all of your business literature. Good copywriting engrosses the readers and takes them on a pleasant trip.

Take Away This: *You need to be creative to be a good copywriter. Work on it.*

Chapter 49

BORROW CREDIBILITY

Until you give solid evidence to back up your claims, your visitors will not believe what you are saying. A lot of people are very skeptical of big claims because the personal element of selling is absent in online marketing.

You have to beg, borrow and steal your way to increase conversions. Borrow credibility from someone who is seen as a credible source. Brand associations, endorsements, testimonials, and certifications can be borrowed. Very often, borrowing credibility becomes the fastest route to success. Showing endorsements by celebrities and demonstrating brand logos can build your credibility.

It is difficult to get started in a market where you don't have any authority, since no one will easily listen to you. It can be intimidating to step into a market where other websites are filled with testimonials and media mentions.

<u>Below are certain ways to compete when you are a start-up.</u>

➤ Admit the fact that you are a newbie and have no college degree on that particular topic. Even if you don't have hundreds of testimonials, you can lure your visitors in by giving them a unique deal if they commit to writing a testimonial.

➤ Finding an expert to partner with is another good option. You might not have much authority, but teaming up with someone who does can be useful.

➤ Start writing content for authority websites. Write guest posts for the famous blogs in your niche. When you write a post for any authority site, some of their authority rubs on you too.

➤ You can experiment by doing some media interviews, which gives you a 'halo effect'. People start looking at you as a credible source when you get featured in a news story.

All kinds of testimonials, especially video testimonials, are very significant for selling products online. The best testimonials explain in detail how your product or service solved a problem. Social proof is very essential for increased conversions, so you need testimonials.

Emphasizing website features like encryption technology is another effective way to add credibility. Ask your visitors to look for the padlock symbol in their browser window in order to ensure them that they are safe. If you are an affiliate marketer, make sure that your products offer a safety net for customers to fall back on.

Always add social proof statistics to your sales page. Tell visitors about your product's history if it has been around for a couple of years. Another very useful piece of information is the number of sales of the product, because people are predisposed to buy what other people buy.

Take Away This: *Beg, borrow, and steal* your way to increase conversions.

Chapter 50

ACCUMULATE USER REVIEWS

A study conducted by 'Internet Retailer' showed that you can increase your conversions by 76% by simply adding user reviews to your site. Moreover, 'Jupiter research' stated that 77% of consumers read reviews before purchasing anything online.

User reviews are a very powerful tool that accelerates

your site's conversion rates and sometimes even your click-through rates in your SERPs (Search Engine Ranking Pages). Even the amount of reviews matter; a rating of 5 out of 10 stars means a lot more if 50 people have left the review, compared to the very same rating but with only 5 reviews. Many customers are well aware of this fact, and a large number of reviews can increase your conversion rates.

Before gathering user reviews, businesses must make sure that they are noticeable on external review sites and are present across numerous social media channels. Businesses hugely benefit from creating a page dedicated to writing reviews. It can help businesses to start an online community to lure customers and nurture existing leads. Many customers need some amount of prompting and persuasion to write a review.

Engaging with the existing customers and asking them to write a review is a good option. It's very likely that a customer will easily be able to write a review by verifying the business's presence across all the reputed social media channels. Email marketing campaigns that are designed for generating reviews can be very useful. Other than solely relying on existing customers to write reviews, asking site visitors to write a review of their experience can also yield results.

User reviews also have a significant influence on SEO. It's a fresh piece of content that search engines can easily index, and it ultimately enriches the content that you provide in the product description. It further helps you to rank for 'product name review' keywords which are used pretty often in certain niches, while also increasing the rate at which users click on your result.

Take Away This: *Your customers will always help you.*

Chapter 51

PROVIDE PRODUCT FAQ

You might think, "FAQ? I already have that on my site."

Well, then that's good. You can skip this chapter, but there are over 70% ecommerce site owners who don't have a FAQ on their page. It's silly, but it's the truth.

Even if you do have a FAQ section on your site, does it

address all your customer's doubts?

What may seem very obvious to you may not always be the case with your customers. Some questions may seem like common sense to you and not worth explaining, but your customers may not feel the same.

Add a FAQ section that your visitors can easily go through, and check if you already have all the answers for their grueling questions. The more questions you have, the better. You can also have a 'search box' that will help your visitors to search for a particular FAQ.

On your FAQ page, categorize the sections and have separate questions for return policy, payment methods, shipping process, terms and conditions of purchase, discount options, coupon codes, warranties, and so on.

Having a well-defined FAQ section is also a great trust signal. It will demonstrate that you are a professional and sound company that is ready to clarify as many of your customer's doubts as possible.

When a visitor sees informative content on your site, it automatically adds to a website's trust factor, especially when it's on the FAQ page.

If you are able to give answers in great detail to all your customers' frequently asked questions, you will be successful in eliminating a lot of 'walls' that a first time visitor generally puts up.

Always add screenshots, details and shipping company logos (UPS, FedEx, etc.) while working on the FAQ section. Place the FAQ link on the 'header menu' and don't make your visitors search for it. Only the big brands can get away by placing their FAQ page on the footer.

Take Away This: *Solve doubts, convert more customers.*

Chapter 52

EVALUATE YOUR USP

Generally, buyers are of three types, *non-spenders, average spenders* and *big spenders.* If you want to increase your conversion rates, you have to target the right type of spenders.

Ask yourself, if you were a customer who visited your site, why would you buy? What's that 1 thing that attracts you the most?

Evaluate your **unique selling proposition (USP)** to help your customers remember you. Your USP will attract your visitors to your site. Examples of USP are free delivery, low prices, awesome customer service, fast shipping, exclusive products, massive discounts, and so on.

Your USP is what sets you apart from the rest of your competition. If a visitor visits several other sites looking for a particular product, why would they decide to buy from you instead of someplace else?

As a human being, you are remembered because of your personality. It's the same with a company. A company should have some unique traits. You don't have to please everybody who visits your website but only a segment of people. That particular segment will become your future loyal customers.

All companies have an USP, but most of them are unaware of it. Anything that makes your company unique, exclusive and different from the rest is your USP.

Tell your users what your USP is. Shout it out from the rooftop.

I will give you some cool examples:

• **Man Craft** (http://www.mancrates.com) ships items in wooden boxes. You will need a crowbar to open them.

• **Nerd Fitness** (http://www.nerdfitness.com) is a health and fitness sites for nerds!

• **TOMS Shoes** (http://www.toms.com) provides a new pair of shoes to a child in need for every pair you buy.

How do you evaluate your USP?

Be different and follow your heart. Do what you do best. There's actually an USP within your company that you are oblivious to. Try to sit quietly and think for 10 minutes.

A very effective way to figure out your USP is to ask yourself 'why should anybody care about my website?', 'what makes my business different or more significant than others?'

If nothing comes up, talk to your old customers. Ask them why they bought from you in the first place. They will tell you what they liked the most about you and your website. This is your 'Unique Selling Proposition'.

Take Away This: *Be different and be proud.*

Chapter 53

HAVE A SOUND RETURNS POLICY

No, it's not a silly point. You need to read the whole chapter to understand the significance of a 'sound returns policy'. Read on...

Returns are a major issue for customers. With a physical shop, the customer knows where the shop is and they are aware of the fact that to return the product, they simply have to go back to the shop and describe the problem. But, this is a major issue with online businesses. This is more of a concern with clothing and shoes, which people cannot try on before purchasing.

Around 3 weeks ago, I bought a Water Purifier from SnapDeal.com. They are one of the biggest online retailers in my country. They have a 7 days money back guarantee, so I thought it was a safe investment.

Here's what happened to me:

It took them 4 days to deliver the product via an express courier. Then, I called the manufacturing company so that they could send their technicians to fix the water purifier in my kitchen. I called them on their toll-free number, he day I received my product. They sent a technician after 3 days to my residence.

Do you realize that it's already been 7 days....

When he opened the product, he found that there was a manufacturing defect (a tube was broken inside the machine). He said that he will get a replacement within 24 hours and get it fixed. The next day when I called him, he said that it's out of stock and he will contact me within 2 days. I heard the same story after 2 days.

So, I had no other option but to call Snapdeal.com and ask them to replace the product. They said that it's not within the warranty period. I called the manufacturing company and filled a complaint (since it has a 1 year manufacturing warranty). It's been 3 weeks now, and I haven't heard from them either.

My $500 product is lying in my basement. I swore never to buy from snapdeal again. I am in the process of filing a complaint in the consumer forum as well.

But the important thing is, I learnt a valuable lesson to re-verify the return policies before buying a product online.

Some of your visitors have been scammed in the past and they are very cautious about a sound return policy. If you don't have a friendly return policy, they might not even bother to call you and re-verify.

Visitors love sites that have a good returns policy and are more likely to buy from them. Usually, free return shipping is a very good option. People hate paying to simply return things, especially if the mistake is from the retailers' end.

Also give your buyers time to return their product.

Thirty days is very common, but if it takes you thirty days to simply deliver the product, then what is the use of the return policy? Thirty days from the delivery date is a better option.

Take Away This: *Think as a buyer, not as a seller.*

Chapter 54

SELECT A MOBILE RESPONSIVE WEBSITE

The 'Google Mobile Research' has recently shown us that 61% of mobile visitors who go through a bad mobile browsing experience simply move on to a competitor's site.

Mobile responsive websites take the exasperation and resentment out of the web browsing experience by adapting the entire layout and shrinking the content to fit the smartphone's screen resolution. It is much easier to navigate a mobile responsive site, and those companies that upgrade their sites reap greater rewards from mobile conversions.

A recent study by e-Marketer showed that only 15% of all online shoppers navigate through a website on a smartphone, while the remaining 85% shop through a website on a desktop computer. Businesses that have low conversions and are getting a lot of visits from mobile users should consider upgrading to a mobile responsive site.

Social media has greatly influenced the conversion process, especially with the growth of mobile devices with which a large number of users are navigating the internet.

Businesses that come up with constructive techniques to use social media across all plans of actions witness increased conversion rates and a very sound competitive advantage.

More than 60% of internet users use a mobile device to check emails or social media sites like Facebook and twitter.

If you are using *email marketing* and *social media* to drive traffic to your website without a responsive design, then you are losing more money than you think.

You can easily get a responsive theme for $50 (if you are

using wordpress) or hire a developer for $200-300 to do it for you. (http://fireyourmentor.com/theme-forest)

Take Away This: *Mobile is the future.*

Chapter 55

INFORM THE CUSTOMER EVERY STEP OF THE WAY

According to a study, ecommerce sites that have implemented this technique have not only increased conversions from repeated customers, but they have also seen an increase of new customers.

How did that happen?

Well, your old customers will post reviews and feedbacks on sites like Yelp, Facebook and Twitter. Your conversions from referrals will drastically increase if you have enough positive press going around on the internet.

When a customer buys something, they are very keen to know when the product is going to arrive at their doorstep. After all, people are impatient. Informing them about an approximate delivery date during check-out is a great start. Try emailing your customers when you dispatch their products. If you are using a delivery service, it's wise to give your customers a tracking number. Notify the user at every step of the process, about as much as you can.

This will greatly improve your conversion rates. If the customers are happy with your service, they are most likely to speak favorably about you. They may recommend you to their family, friends or colleagues and probably buy from you again.

There is a greater chance that people will again buy from someone who had informed them of every little development and answered all their questions rather than from someone who completely ignored their concerns and kept them in the dark. A company that shows that it cares for its customers even after they have finished purchasing will make their customers happier and far more likely to return.

Take Away This: *Customers like to stay informed.*

Chapter 56

PRICE ANCHORING

STARTER	STANDARD	ADVANCED	CORPORATE
$1495 PER MONTH	$2486 PER MONTH	$3997 PER MONTH	$12000 PER MONTH

Price anchoring has been successfully used by tons of people in the past, and they all swear by its benefits. Let me explain what price anchoring actually means.

It's a pricing strategy that enables you to create an 'Anchor Price' or a 'Stop Price'. It's usually the highest possible price for a certain range of products.

Let's say, you own a furniture store and you have office chairs starting from $50 to $150.

You will start noticing that you often sell chairs that are

worth $60-$100. You will make very limited sales for a chair that's worth $150.

Now, here's an easy way to sell more high-end chairs.

You can get a chair that's worth $500 and use it as an 'Anchor Price'. Place it on the front door, right where people can effortlessly see it when they visit your store. When they see a chair worth $500 and then explore the rest of your store where you have chairs worth $50-$100, these chairs will appear much cheaper, as you have already created an anchor price in their sub-conscious mind.

This will ultimately result in more people buying a chair worth $150 as they will start considering it a cheap bargain.

There's another way to use 'price anchoring'.

Let's take this example:

You were searching for an antivirus software and you found this great software that almost guarantees you that your system will never catch a virus. They also have reviews to back them up.

Instance 1:
You find that they have priced it at $400. Almost 90% of visitors would search for a cheaper alternative.

Instance 1:
You find that they have priced it at $700 but they were offering a deal of $300 off.

It's still costly, but the bounce rate will reduce from 90%.

Note that the term 'expensive item' is invalid. It's valid or arguable only when it's compared to a cheaper product.

Take Away This: *Being expensive is relative to a cheaper price.*

Chapter 57

TEST YOUR PRODUCTS

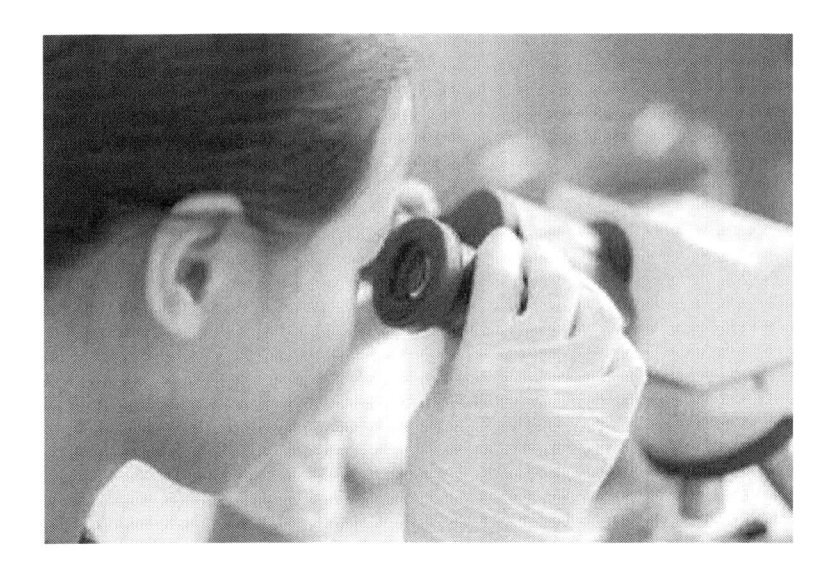

Has it ever occurred to you that you have a great product, but nobody's willing to pay?

I have seen a lot of people crying about the fact that they have built a great product but nobody is willing to buy. In fact, the conversion ratio is so poor sometimes, that they had to file bankruptcy.

The reason is, it's a great product for you, but for your customers, it may not be as interesting as you think it is.

If you are into affiliate marketing and drop-shipping,

never sell a product without personally testing it. It might seriously affect your brand image if you have not tested the product yourself.

If you are offering an online service, here are a few things you need to consider:

- Build a Beta Launch
- Run surveys to get an idea of your target audience
- Ask for feedbacks and suggestions from your beta users
- Ask for recommendations from your beta users

An important thing that you need to realize is that creating a website is a cakewalk and building a product is easy, but selling it is difficult.

If you build a product or service after investing thousands of dollars, you are doing it wrong. Never invest money on something without testing it first.

If you are planning to create a software for a certain audience, such as educational institutions, contact these institutions and pitch your idea. Offer them big discounts and persuade them to buy upfront. If you get a significant amount of customers who are willing to pay upfront (even before the product is ready), go ahead with your idea and build it. That way, you can at least be assured that it's going to sell in the future and your investments won't go down the drain.

As a customer, if you dearly love a product idea and you know for sure that it would be instrumental in solving an ongoing problem, won't you pay upfront to get the product built?

Use your website as the single biggest marketing tool. If you are coming up with a new product, inform your customers beforehand. Let them know what you are up to.

Add a 'Pop Up' or an 'Opt In' form where they are required to fill in their details, in order to notify them when you finally launch your product. You can also ask them to grab an offer of '70% Discount' by paying upfront. The possibilities are endless.

Take Away This: *Test first, build later.*

Chapter 58

REFLECT PEOPLE'S EXPECTATIONS

When you were a little child, you expected gifts on your birthday. When you didn't get one, how did you react?

Each and every visitor comes to your website or blog with an expectation. You need to reflect that same expectation and help them to solve their problem. You need to live up to their expectations.

If you are running a gift shop during Christmas or any other festive occasion, people will come to your website expecting some discounts or special offers. If you don't live up to their expectation, they will go looking for it somewhere else.

It's not just about selling a product or a service. Let's say, you are running a blog that publishes new, innovative and unique children's stories with the help of a network of guest authors.

So, when parents or even children visit your blog, they will expect to read a new story every time. If you have not updated your blog in a month, you will most definitely lose a lot of readers in the due process.

You will find a lot of expectations that are quite common with your audience. As a matter of fact, they are very basic expectations. Yet, a lot of website owners never bother to sit down and think what their customers really expect when they enter their site.

Do they want to see a large pop-up banner? 'Definitely not'.

Do they want to see a live-help button and a phone number? 'Definitely yes'.

By the time you complete this book, you will become more cognizant of your customer's expectations.

Identify your niche and ascertain what your audience expects. Try to relate to them and reflect the same with your website. If you can make a connection with your audience, they will revert back.

Take Away This: *Fulfill expectations, or they will leave.*

Chapter 59

ELIMINATE FRICTION WORDS

People will love your website if you tell them what they want to hear. Similarly, they will also leave your website when you ask them to do something that they are not willing to do.

On a personal level, would you be friends with someone who is sharp-tongued? A person who keeps nagging you incessantly with his irritating voice?

"There's a way of saying things". It's a well-known proverb. It also applies to all your website's visitors. You need to master the art of conveying your message to them.

There are friction words that can act as a barrier between you and your readers. You need to sugar coat your friction words or replace them with other pleasant words.

Instead of saying, 'Sign up on my blog', you can say 'Count me in' on your opt-in form. Similarly, if you are selling them something, instead of saying 'Buy Now', you can say 'Join Now' or 'Start Now'.

Words that tell people what to do are friction words. Generally, these are things that people are not interested in. These words create cognitive friction.

A site that converts focuses on what people want to do. Very often, calls to action are filled with friction words. These words confuse, irritate and frustrate the readers. With the right set of skills, you can easily reduce the number of these friction words, make the conversion process more user-friendly and procure more revenue.

Take Away This: *Speak as you want to be spoken to.*

Chapter 60

OVERRIDE ALL RISKS

What's your greatest fear when you shop online? For me, it's mostly, the fear of wasting my money on a substandard product or the item not matching the description.

Most people have similar fears. When you think from their point of view, these are huge risks for them. You need to minimize their risks at all cost.

If a person fears that he might lose money on a substandard product, offer him a 30 days money back guarantee. If someone fears that he might not receive the exact item as described, offer them a clear return policy.

These simple steps that you take to diminish your customer's risks will help you to convert them better.

Potential customers will never buy from you if they have even 1% of their doubt remaining about your product and work structure. Even tackling 99% of the total risk factors won't do you any good. You need to solve 100% of it.

Here's a question:

A brand new mobile company is offering their stunning range of latest android phones for just $50. Will you ever buy an android phone from this new company if you have even the slightest doubt that it can be a cheap Chinese phone?

You definitely won't buy it. You will rather buy from one of the reputed phone companies that you trust.

Now, go to your website and see what you have done to override the risks held by your customers. Try to visit your website as a customer who is planning to buy a certain product from your website. Go through the buying process by selecting a product, adding it to the cart, and filling in the details. Now, try to think like a customer.

What's your biggest fear (risk) before you enter your credit card details?

Take Away This: *Customers hate the risk factor.*

Chapter 61

ANNOUNCE THE PROBLEM

Human beings are often not aware of a problem until they are told about it.

I never had a problem with my old 21-inch LCD TV until my wife told me to get a 55-inch LED TV. Now, I can't watch TV on a small screen.

It happens with every one of us. We are unaware about a

lot of things because we are so used to our old, comfortable habits. People hate change.

A visitor comes to a website in search of a solution or remedy. However, at times, he might not be aware of his own problem. Therefore, it's your job to announce the problem loudly and clearly on your homepage.

For instance, you are randomly surfing through Facebook in the evening and you see an ad that says, "You are losing customers on your website".

Once you realize that they have pointed out your 'problem', you will click that link. You now feel that you are facing a serious problem with your sales or conversions, and you need a solution or a way to fix it.

You were not even aware of 'this problem' prior to encountering the ad. Now, suddenly you want to learn more about increasing your conversions.

I recently ordered a book from Kindle on "How to price a Kindle Book".

Initially, I had no real intention of buying it. I was just surfing through the Amazon Kindle store and checking out various categories for my own book.

I had a problem that I was trying to solve. I was ready to publish this book, but I didn't know how to price it correctly. So, as soon as I noticed this book, I bought it.

Your customers and visitors might give very little thought about their existing problems. Most of them are not even aware of it. You need to announce their problem loudly and clearly.

The next time you buy an antivirus online, you will notice that the 'Antivirus Companies' have stated the 'virus problem' vividly. Some rapacious companies even go as far as publishing fake pop-ups that say, "Your computer is infected with malware". It sends a clear message that you need to avail their services to get rid of your virus issues.

Take Away This: *Point out a problem and offer a solution.*

Chapter 62

SERVE YOUR SOLUTION

Once you have clearly defined their problem, the next thing you need to do is offer a solution that's impossible to resist.

Last year, I suffered a malware attack on around 20 of my

websites. I wanted to immediately pay a hefty amount to resolve the issue. Normally, I wait and take some time to contemplate, but I couldn't afford to do that this time.

Later, I realized that there were many invisible factors that were pushing me to spend an exorbitant amount to solve my problem.

They were:

1. Urgency of the situation. I was losing traffic on my sites.
2. Worth/Value of my loss. It was a lot more than what I was actually willing to spend.
3. Panic, anxiety, immense tension and stress. Psychological factors.

So, while defining a problem and offering a solution, you need to explain the urgency of your situation to your potential customers. You need to make them aware of their loss. It's a small price they will be paying to solve their problem.

Do you have a product that's solution-driven? If yes, then write down the problem and a solution. Build a sales copy and mention the problem as well as the solution. Until you tell them via a sales copy (both headline and content body), they won't know that you have the inventory to solve their problem.

If you have multiple products, then try to find out how each product can be effective in solving a particular micro-problem.

Take Away This: *Show them the magic potion.*

Chapter 63

CLARITY TRUMPS PERSUASION

"Stop trying to over-persuade people. Be clear."

It's a pivotal lesson that you should learn before writing for the web.

When you check out sites like www.buzzbundle.com, you know exactly what I am talking about. The website is really easy to understand. They have just enough information for a layman to comprehend, without making it too complex or too advertorial.

When you visit a restaurant, would you prefer a simple menu or a complex one? It's the same with your website. The more clarity you bring to your content, the better you connect with your readers.

How to bring more clarity?

It's simple. Just eliminate all unnecessary items from your website.

The other day, I consulted an ecommerce site owner who sells toys. On the check-out page where he collects customer's names and shipping addresses, he also had a space to enter the company's details. He doesn't need a tax invoice with the company's details, so there was no point in asking for it.

Similarly, once you try and eliminate all unnecessary items from your texts, ads or images, you will bring more clarity to your website.

No matter how much you persuade people to buy a product, they will never buy it unless all their doubts are cleared away. The only way to make them pull out their credit cards is by giving them absolute knowledge about a product or a service.

Tell them clearly what they can expect from you, and at the same time, assure them that they are in good hands. Show them the product specifications, features, testimonials and other descriptions. Be as clear as possible.

If you have ever visited a sales page of any of the 'clickbank' products, you might have already noticed that their sales pages exceed over 3000 words. I personally found them very informative and instructive; research shows that they perform 300% better than product descriptions that are limited to only 500 words.

Their lengthy and profound sales pages are a crucial factor behind their stupendous success rates.

Take Away This: *Be crystal clear.*

Chapter 64

HIRE A VISUAL DESIGNER

A visual designer will help you to create and publish stunning visuals on your website. If you have budgetary concerns, you can access platforms like fiverr.com, where you only need to pay $5.

"People believe what they see rather than what they read."

"A picture speaks a thousand words."

There are numerous such quotes on how important or significant an image is.

You can check sites like Getresponse.co.uk . Study the graphics of their notebooks and phones. Their images and graphics encompass and express everything that they offer. They didn't have to write a 3000-word sales page to entice their visitors, because their graphics alone are visually gratifying. Do you think a poor quality graphic would have delivered the same excellence?

At the same time, you will have to think about your website speed. If you upload un-optimized, very high-quality graphics, they will slow down your website. You need to balance quality and size of an image. A visual graphic designer can take care of both these factors.

You need a professional visual designer who is creative enough to connect to your website visitors. Consider it an investment and not an expense. Hire one today, if you don't have one already.

Leave this work to an expert so that you can focus on other important tasks in your business.

Take Away This: *You need somebody more creative than you are.*

Chapter 65

BE SPECIFIC

Be specific about the single most important feature of your product or service. What's your unique selling proposition? Be specific to your buyers on what you offer instead of beating around the bush.

People come with less time to visit your website, as I have already told you in the beginning of this book. You need to be dead simple and very specific.

Example: If you are selling an antivirus software via your

site, you need to tell your visitors that it removes any and every virus that's available on the internet. Your buyers are not interested in knowing about the different features of your antivirus. All they care about is removing viruses from their computer using an antivirus. It's as simple as that.

How can you be more specific?

You need to think about that one solution that your product offers to your customers. Forget about features for a moment.

If you sell winter clothes, then the main objective is to provide warmth. If you sell business cards, then the chief purpose is to make an impression, and so on.

People mostly visit online stores to browse or surf rather than to buy. Most don't even spend 8 seconds on a site if they find it boring or worthless.

Whereas, when a customer enters your physical store, they spend at least 15-20 minutes flicking through your products, even if they have no intention of buying.

The only way to grab your customer's attention is by being more specific. Try to make them stay on your site for more than 5 minutes. They can read about the features later when they make a decision to compare and buy an item from your store.

Take Away This: *You have 5 seconds to tell them what* *you offer.*

Chapter 66

BE EXCLUSIVE

There are many reputed brands like eBay and Amazon with tons of highly regarded sellers.

Why should your visitors buy from you and not from any of your competitors?

You see, online buyers are always researching about different features, pricing and promos. You need to be exclusive if you want to convert a potential buyer to a customer.

If you aren't exclusive and don't offer generalized products and services, your potential buyers will just surf through your website and bounce to the next website.

The big question is, how to be more exclusive?

It's simple. Offer exclusive deals.

Tomorrow, if I plan to buy a laptop, I would visit eBay and find a power seller. But, if I find a 'new' website that offers free softwares and an extended 5 years warranty along with my purchase, I would definitely choose them over a power seller.

It is difficult to buy products from a brand new site. Personally, I wouldn't buy from a new site because I need assurance that it isn't a faulty product and I also fear the item being overpriced.

The moment the new website offered a 5 years extended warranty, they eliminated all my doubts.

However, things differ from one industry to another. If you manufacture mobile phones, you can easily become exclusive by offering free apps with your phone. If you are in the clothing line, you should sell a fabric that's rare and limited. If you are in the beauty industry, you can become more exclusive by offering big combo offers. If you sell books, then you can be exclusive by offering a free course or a tutorial to all your readers. Again, the possibilities are endless.

Take Away This: *Be so good that it's hard to resist.*

Chapter 67

USE TRIGGERS BELOW THE CTA BUTTON

Most Popular!

Click Here To Join Today For Just $95/mo
no contracts, no commitments, cancel whenever you like

Now, what's a trigger? It's actually a text just below the video that will solve a doubt that comes to a buyer's mind just before making a purchase.

If I buy something tomorrow, I might feel, "How long will it take to deliver the product?"

A smart marketer will put a trigger like this just below the buy now button. You will notice that "Delivery within 48 hrs." is a trigger in this case.

BUY NOW >
Delivery within 48 hrs.

There can be other triggers such as :

- Save money
- Risk-free
- Save time
- Money back guarantee
- Offer end in 4 hrs.

If you still don't have a trigger, use one. Try split testing and see what converts best for your business.

The biggest challenge can be to identify your customer's doubts. You can either take a survey or ask your friends to go through the check-out process and get their feedback.

I use Usabilityhub to create small tests. It's a free and easy way to understand what triggers to use. (http://fireyourmentor.com/usabilityhub)

So what happens when you don't use a trigger?

You might not lose many visitors if you don't use a trigger, but there can be a segment of potential customers who will not convert. A trigger will act as a bridge to connect a customer who is in doubt, especially during the check-out process.

Take Away This: *A gun isn't the only thing with a trigger.*

Chapter 68

GET A PROFESSIONAL LOGO

This is perhaps the most basic lesson when it comes to writing for the web. A logo determines whether your website is a professional website or not.

More than 80% of the website-owners who come to me for consultation are without a professional logo. It doesn't make sense to not invest in building your brand.

Do you have a professional logo?

If you just have text with the name of your website or brand, it looks totally unprofessional. Maybe you haven't even realized it. Try doing a survey if you doubt it. Trust me, 90% of your visitors will say that it doesn't look professional.

There's a marketplace called seoclerks.com. I found some amazing logo designers for $5-$50.

When a visitor comes to your website and doesn't see a logo, there's very little chances of him pulling out his credit card and using it on your site. Think about it; would you use your credit card on a website that doesn't have a logo?

You might argue that you aren't selling anything via your website. You have a simple blog. Well, with a blog, your conversions are calculated by the number of emails you capture. People will be unwilling to give you their email addresses if they don't trust you. You need to do every possible thing to gain their trust and confidence. Remember, you are competing against a million other websites that are doing exactly the same thing. What makes you stand out from the rest?

It's a 1 time investment. Once you have a logo, you can use it everywhere to build your brand. You can use it during guest posting, on your t-shirt, on your car, while doing a press release, on your company's diary, and on your calendar. The possibilities of promoting your brand are endless.

Take Away This: *A logo makes a brand.*

Chapter 69

LEVERAGE THE CONVENIENCE FACTOR

You can sell the same product and get your clients to pay you more. Want to know how? Read on...

Research has shown that people pay extra if you provide them 'comfort' and 'convenience'.

Example: When you order food for delivery from a Chinese restaurant, it will cost you a bit more than the usual price. You are still comfortable and pay that extra money happily.

Okay, let me ask you a question:

Will you pay $50 for a taxi that stops at your doorstep, or $45 for a taxi that stops 100 meters away from your home? Obviously, you will choose to pay $50 and get out at your doorstep, irrespective of the fact that you can cover 100 meters in just two minutes on foot.

You can leverage the same 'convenience factor' to earn more money from your product. However, you will need to decide how you can take advantage of it.

People have started shopping online for the same 'convenience factor'. They don't have to drive through traffic and waste the whole day to buy a small product. It takes them 5 minutes to research and place an order online.

Time + Energy = Convenience

Here's what I used to do when I sold SEO services:

- I offered 24 hours delivery for an extra $xx.
- I offered extra add-ons for better results.
- I offered to do the keyword research myself for an extra $xx.

Implement 'convenience factor' into your copywriting. Use it in your headline and content. Find out how you can help your customers to save time and energy.

<u>Take Away This</u>: *People pay for comfort.*

Chapter 70

WRITE SHORT SENTENCES AND PARAGRAPHS

> **A screenshot from socialtriggers.com**
>
> **The Six Degrees of Separation**
>
> Have you heard the expression "Six degrees of separation?" If yes, bear with me a sec.
>
> Long story short, six degrees of separation is the theory that everyone is six (or fewer) steps away from anyone in the world.
>
> That means, a friend of a friend of a friend of a friend of a friend is Bill Gates. Or Warren Buffett. Or Justin Bieber.
>
> So, if you become the person your friends want to introduce to their friends, you can literally meet anyone.
>
> Just imagine how GREAT that would be for getting ahead in your business or career.
>
> The question is, how can you become that person?

I wanted to include this point in the very beginning, but I stopped myself. Why? Because it's a very simple idea that many people are aware of; as such, I think that around 80% of my readers would have ignored it, thinking that they already know it.

If I were to take away 1 point out of all the 70 points, this would be it. "Write short sentences and paragraphs". Believe me, this technique is extremely powerful, and it will increase your conversions dramatically.

Around 90% of your readers will never read the 3rd sentence if the first 2 sentences are too long and uninteresting. Analyze your bounce rate with Google analytics by doing a simple experiment with two articles.

Write an article with short sentences and paragraphs. Write another article on a similar topic with long sentences and long paragraphs. Then, compare the time spent by visitors on each article with the help of Google Analytics.

While writing an article for your website or blog, keep these points in mind.

1. The first two paragraphs should have 1 sentence each.
2. Start writing 4-5 sentences from the 3rd paragraph onwards.

The first sentence should be attention grabbing. It should have around 8-15 words (but no more than that). It should also give a sense of exhilaration, anticipation and thrill to the reader. He or she will then proceed to the 2nd sentence, which should be short as well. These first two paragraphs will only have one sentence each.

Once you are done with the first two paragraphs, try not to include more than 6 sentences in the rest of your paragraphs.

The same applies for when you write an email. If you can get a person to read your first 3 sentences, then he will probably read the rest of your content.

Take Away This: *Make them read the 3rd sentence.*

CONCLUSION

I hope you have enjoyed reading this book. I have tried to offer as much knowledge as possible with this little book.

Use this book as a reference while working on any new landing page or a website. Verify that you have implemented at least 70% of what's been written in this book.

This book will act as a constant reminder for you, whenever you publish a new landing page or a website. Most people overlook these points; try not to be one of them.

I have something more for you....

Every book that a reader buys is an investment and not an expense. If you can get back your investment with some profit after reading a book, it's a winner.

After reading this book, you will earn much more than what you have invested

Since this is my first book, I would like to make a personal connection with all my readers who have put their faith in me and my work.

My consultancy fee is $125/hr, but I want to offer you something for free.

So, here's an opportunity to <u>contact me directly and ask me 2 questions</u> related to your website. You can ask me anything related to internet marketing, and I will try to answer them to the best of my knowledge.

Fill in this form to ask me.:

http://fireyourmentor.com/ask-me

I will publish my next 2 books within 2-3 months.

1. 70 Secrets Revealed: Do Your Own SEO Better than 'SEO Experts'
2. 70 Secrets Revealed: Social Media Strategies That Nobody Will Teach You.

I will offer it for $0.99 to all my readers during the launch day. To get notified about the launch, sign up to my mailing list. *(I hate spam as much as you do).*

http://www.fireyourmentor.com/70-secrets-revealed/

Before you leave, I have a humble request

Since this is my first book, I might have committed some errors. Please forgive me for that.

I need your valuable feedback. If, by any chance, you are disappointed with my book, please let me know directly via my personal email: harsh@fireyourentor.com . I will work on your feedback and fix my mistakes on my updated version.

If you are happy with this book, feel free to share it with your friends, family, audience, fans and followers.

I will be obliged if you leave a **positive review**. I want nothing more than a happy and content reader.

I wish you all the success in your business.

Take care, stay in touch.

-Harsh

Website: FireYourMentor.com

Twitter: @jr_sci

FB Page: https://www.facebook.com/FireYourMentor

IMAGE CREDITS: Via freedigitalphotos.net

The images were designed/created by Boians Cho Joo Young, jesadaphorn, digitalart, ratch0013, chanpipat, potowizard, luigi diamanti, Ambro, Master isolated images, photostock, jscreationzs, stockimages,bplanet, nongpimmy, phanlop88, sumetho, pat138241, Stuart Miles, nuttakit, vectorolie, cooldesign, graur razvan ionut, ratch0013, photokanok, pakorn, David Castillo Dominici, watcharakun, bplanet, nokhoog_buchachon, africa.

Printed in Poland
by Amazon Fulfillment
Poland Sp. z o.o., Wrocław